MW01104676

Rescued by Love

God's mercy on the streets of Vancouver

Stories of women who left the
world of prostitution

By Bernice S. Sondrup

Table of Contents

Forward

by Pastor Ernie Culley
Senior Pastor: Agape Life Center Community Church,
Vancouver, BC Canada

Into The Darkness

Not long after arriving in Vancouver in the late 1980's I began to notice a number of women standing on the sidewalks of our city, soliciting the passing drivers. It dawned on me that these were sex trade workers. As I was pastoring a large inner city church, I did the typical pastoral "guilt shift shuffle" and told the congregation that "someone" needed to do something about reaching out to these precious people who obviously needed Jesus. The congregation looked at me like the proverbial "tree full of owls," with a collective, "Who? Me? Expression on their face, and not one volunteered. A few days later one of them brought me an article from the local Christian newspaper that described the efforts of a former pimp, now converted, who had launched an outreach to this very group. Volunteers were solicited, I made the call, and as they say, the rest is history.

I was invited out on a Monday evening to join the outreach team, and thus began twenty plus years of reaching out with the compassion of Jesus to some of the most interesting people I've ever met.

Virtually every Monday night when there was no schedule conflict would find me with a very diverse collection of individuals. With hot chocolate and booklets in hand, walking "the stroll" of Hastings and Cordova Street, as well as various other neighbourhoods where the women would occasionally work.

In those years we have witnessed breathtakingly dramatic

transformation, as well as heartbreaking tragedies. As a pastor, when I survey a Sunday morning congregation and see a precious young woman, hands raised in worship to Jesus, and remember the first time I spoke to her she was on a dark street corner, selling herself for a few dollars to support a drug addiction, now with tears of joy on her face, and realize I had a role in the transformation, feel it validates my whole life and ministry.

I will be forever grateful to the Crossfire ministry team for launching me into such an incredibly rewarding urban mission field.

Pastor Ernie Culley

Introduction

The stories in this book, represent God's love and mercy;
in transforming lives. The names of the people have been
changed to protect their privacy. Most if these events took
place in Vancouver BC from 1988 to 2002.
I am still in contact with many of the women, it is a privilege
to see the growth in their lives and relationship with God.

Bernice Sondrup

Chapter 1

Embracing the Challenges

Listening to his words, I felt awkward and uncomfortable. It felt like the preacher was speaking to me face-to-face. As he read from Colossians 3:1-17, the Holy Spirit convicted me of my poor choices. I knew I was living a self-centered life that separated me from God.

During my mid-teens, I came to know Jesus as my Lord and Saviour. It happened the same evening my sister, Verna, was baptized. However, my new found faith was in complete opposition to my Dad's aspirations for my life. Angry with me, he did all he could to discourage me from being a Christian. Eventually relenting, I turned away from God and once again chose to live for myself. I was, however, still always aware of God's presence surrounding me. Occasionally, I would attend church but never felt like I belonged.

Here I was again, five years later, being invited back into relationship with my heavenly Father. Verna was closest to me of all my siblings; she'd asked her Christian friends to pray for me. Through their diligent prayers and her bull-dog persistence in asking me to attend church, I finally came to this special outreach gathering.

My brother and his wife, who weren't Christians, were also going to attend, so I felt obliged to come. At the meeting, we sat together. I felt like an absolute hypocrite as my brother and sister in-law knew I wasn't living for God.

When the preacher gave an altar call, I asked my brother and his wife if they wanted to go up to the front with me. They declined. My heart was broken; I had no right to invite them into relationship with the Lord when my own life was a mess. I had been in rebellion towards God. Instead of going forward for prayer at the outreach service, I ran to the washroom and wept bitterly. With tears streaming down my face, I prayed and recommitted my life wholeheartedly to God. My life now belonged to Jesus Christ.

The Call

I was born to a working class family in Vancouver, BC—the fifth of six children. Growing up, we were loved and well cared for by my parents. Eager to build my self-confidence, they continually reminded me there was nothing I couldn't accomplish in life. This helped me tremendously in my ministry work, and to steadfastly pursue God's purposes for my life.

Paul and I were married on February 18, 1961. The following year, we both enrolled at Vancouver Bible College. The classes were very enjoyable. Like a sponge I absorbed all I learnt, I couldn't get enough of God's word or spend enough time in His presence. On my walk to campus one day, I heard him say, "Bernice, I am preparing you to win souls for me." At first, I didn't fully understand, however, as I continued my studies it became clear—bringing people into relationship with God was my life's calling.

Skid Row Encounters

While attending Vancouver Bible College, every student was required to join an outreach ministry. Much to my dismay, I was assigned to the Street Ministry Team. It had nothing to do with my strengths and abilities or so I thought. I had simply signed up too late for a more 'comfortable' option like ministering to children. Even though I was terrified of skid row and petrified of drunks and violence, God in His infinite wisdom placed me exactly where he wanted me to be. I had no idea that he was preparing me for my future vocation!

The team met weekly at the corner of Carroll and Cordova Streets.

11

Our brave band of students consisted of ten to twelve young adults with a small pump organ, lots of faith and the expectation of bringing others into relationship with God. The majority of the people who gathered around to hear the gospel were men. That year, over thirty men and one woman received Jesus as their Lord and Saviour. It was during this time, I encountered a prostitute for the first time—her name was Wanda. From that day forward, God birthed a ministry to prostitutes in my heart.

A Girl Called Wanda

To make ends meet, Wanda labored on fishing boats during the day, and worked on the streets at night. Although she was average in height, blond haired and blue eyed, she exuded a tough feisty character. Even men were afraid of her!

One night, as she strolled past our team, she stopped to listen. I spotted her and immediately moved closer. As I began to talk to her, she brushed me off and hastily disappeared. A few weeks later while our team was preaching, Wanda once again entered the crowd. She was earnestly listening to the message. Near the end of the preaching she walked over to me. We talked a bit about her job on the fishing boats but she didn't refer to her other job as a prostitute. Over several months, we slowly built a relationship. Wanda was willing to hear the gospel but wasn't ready to be a Christian. I told her if she ever wanted to talk, I'd be happy to chat over coffee. "Yeah, maybe someday," she replied indifferently.

A Call Came from Grace Hospital

Wanda had been in an accident and was in bad shape. She wanted to see me. Hospitals aren't my favorite places to visit but I knew God wanted me to go. The corridors smelling of antiseptic were dimly lit. I went to the nurse's desk and asked for directions. Winding through the wards, I found her room and cautiously entered. It was dark and eerie. The only light in the room came from a small window behind her bed. I could hardly see her in the bed. Once my eyes adjusted, I was stunned. Her face was covered in bandages. She had a leg in a cast hoisted by a pulley, and her upper body was wrapped in a cast. As I drew closer, she recognized me and murmured, "Thank you for coming." I sat down and asked her what happened.

Tearfully, she recounted the incident. Three men had demanded that she work for them. She refused but they were not willing to accept "no" for an answer. They had a syringe with heroin in it and were forcefully about to inject her. Panicking, she jumped out the window. She broke through a store awning, landing three floors below on the sidewalk. This resulted in her broken back, broken leg and multiple lacerations.

Wanda knew that God had spared her life. Sobbing profusely, she asked Jesus to become her Lord and Saviour. She also prayed a prayer of repentance to turn away from prostitution, and from living for herself.

During her hospital stay, I visited several times. We shared many Bible studies and discussed her future. After several months she was well enough to leave. Terrified of living in Vancouver, she returned to her hometown, Kimberly, BC. My last visit was tearful, yet joyful. We said our farewells at the hospital. When she arrived home, she wrote several times. In all her letters, she described how grateful she was that the Lord had changed her life. It took a dramatic incident to wake her up but she was thankful for the intervention.

A Fish on Dry Land

Following our graduation from Vancouver Bible College, my husband Paul went on to complete the Wycliffe Bible Translator's course at the University of Oklahoma. In November 1963, God opened a door for us to minister to the Shuswap Indians in the Cariboo of British Columbia.

Over the next decade, our three children, Philip, JoAnn and Beverly were born. As I spent time with our First Nation sisters, the Lord gave me an abounding love and compassion for some of the women who endured ongoing domestic abuse. Our missionary work in the Cariboo is a whole story on its own, to be told at another time. Unfortunately, we had to resign in 1973 due to Paul developing a chronic illness. I found this difficult because I'd grown to love the Shuswap people as my own family.

After moving to Vancouver Island, we purchased a gas station and grocery store at Fanny Bay. This was a very dark season in my life. My heart was breaking because I was a vocational missionary out of a job, a fish on dry land.

Three years later, we relocated to Vancouver, BC. Paul was unable to sustain a consistent income to support our family. As our financial situation grew desperate, I was compelled into becoming the breadwinner. God blessed me with a stable job as the Food Services Manager of a seniors' home.

Although the work was enjoyable, my heart yearned to be a vocational missionary again. One Sunday, there was a stirring message at church that focused on sharing the gospel in our city. My heart was aching to respond. While driving home, I cried out, "Lord I want to serve you as a missionary again!" I heard his resounding reply, "Bernice, you have NEVER stopped being a missionary."

Stepping Into a World of Darkness

In addition to my work at the seniors' home, I continued to seek God as to how else I could serve Him. I enrolled in a Prayer Counseling course at our church and took a counseling program with a Christian Crisis Hot line called Telecare. While volunteering at Telecare, I realized there were hundreds of confused despondent people in the Greater Vancouver area.

A year later, my brother, Clifford called. He'd launched an urban outreach to prostitutes called Crossfire Ministries[2]. He asked if I would be interested in joining. Because I was especially fearful of Vancouver's Downtown East-side, I didn't respond hastily. As I prayed, the Lord reminded me that His guiding hand was with me so I made arrangements to join the ministry team on Monday nights.

Clifford introduced me to my street ministry partner, a young woman named Margaret. She was fearless of Vancouver's skid row residents. We strategically meandered down a dark alley where many women were plying their trade. This was a terrifying experience for me. My heart was pounding; I'd never been so afraid in my entire life! However, something supernatural took place as I remained in the vicinity. My fears began to melt away as I looked into the eyes of the disoriented, lonely individuals passing by. Margaret was so patient, kind and gentle with each person we encountered. They listened to her as she chatted with them and thanked her for caring. By the time we'd finished our route that evening, I knew this was where God wanted me to serve. After arriving home, I wept with compassion for the women who sold themselves as prostitutes.

Burning Out

Despite the late nights, I assisted Crossfire Ministries on a part-time basis for ten years. It was often difficult to shake off the horrific stories, the depressed faces and the spiritual darkness I sensed as we ministered in this dilapidated neighborhood. It became challenging to get up in the mornings, send my children off to school and thrust myself into my day job.

Ultimately, the missions work became overwhelming. In addition to ministering on the streets and mentoring women, I facilitated an addictions recovery group. I also managed a safe house, and was given the role as Secretary-Treasurer on the Board of Directors at Crossfire Ministries. Burnout set in. The conflict of holding a full-time job and serving as a part-time missionary was too stressful. Exhausted, I had to either give up my work with Crossfire Ministries or leave my job at the seniors' home.

Adventures With God

Paul and I earnestly brought this dilemma before God. We both felt that I should relinquish being a Food Services Manager, to once again be a full-time missionary. This was not an easy decision. Due to his deteriorating health, Paul had been obliged to take an early retirement.

Crossfire Team & Van

It meant that I'd be walking away from a steady income plus benefits. As a family, we had to step out in faith and trust the Lord to meet our day-to-day requirements.

In October 1997, I joined the full-time staff at Crossfire Ministries. The leaders of our church supported the decision we made. God never allowed us to become poverty stricken or destitute. Throughout the five years I worked full-time at Crossfire, our heavenly Father always provided all the finances and health care we ever needed.

Being a full-time missionary was exhilarating and a great privilege. I could focus 100% on the work ahead. Each day was filled with new adventures! Having more time to minister, I developed stronger relationships with the women I met. Furthermore, I could establish a weekly daytime drop-in center, and had time to take a course in Substance Abuse Counseling—a great benefit to my work at the Safe House.

Chapter 2

Moonlit Evenings

Starting out at Crossfire Ministries I didn't always know what I was doing. However, I knew God was completely in control. All I had to do was show up, and He would do the rest.

Monday evenings were designated for street outreach. For safety reasons we always worked with a ministry partner. Going out in pairs, we were assigned to a specific zone where we met people. As we ministered, our team leader drove around the neighborhood and checked in on us.

Spiritual Wars

Working in the Downtown East-side at night was dangerous and volatile. Situations could become explosive at any given moment. I had no doubt that we were constantly fighting brutal spiritual forces. Before gathering on the streets, we would fervently pray together. However, the battle often manifested even before we set foot on the streets. I frequently experienced a severe headache or stomach pain just a few hours before leaving home. Nonetheless, after arriving and praying with our ministry team, all the symptoms would miraculously disappear.

For our struggle is not against flesh and blood, but against the rulers, against the authorities, against the powers of this dark world and against the spiritual forces of evil in the heavenly realms (Ephesians 6:12).

I believe that these spiritual forces of evil were making me ill, trying to prevent me from ministering. As these men and women engaged in their chosen life styles, these were the same spiritual enemies that chained them to prostitution, drug and alcohol addictions.

Overcoming my sickness, fatigue and past fears was well worth the effort and fight. My personal motto was, and still is "I love the battle—I will not be defeated, and I will be victorious through Christ Jesus!"

The "Red-Light" Zones

Vancouver had a number of districts where male and female prostitutes street-walked on the lookout for johns. Over the years all these areas have undergone substantial upgrades due to the building of new commercial properties and residential high-rises, and prostitutes have had to find other locations to operate.

"High Track" was located Downtown, around Richards and Davie. It was renowned for the classier, more expensive prostitutes. The ladies here dressed to impress, flaunting glamorous outfits and plush furs.

The transsexuals lingered in the region of Richards and Helmecken. They were cautiously friendly. Their unconventional attire usually included very provocative women's clothing. God would totally transform their lives, once they came to know Jesus as Lord and Saviour. When "Georgina" became a Christian, he immediately changed his name back to "George."

"Low Track" was on Cordova and East Hastings. Police officers patrolling here on the Downtown East-side were especially concerned about the women's safety. The majority of the ladies worked to sustain their drug habits. Accustomed to catching a glimpse of us, the police would regularly encourage our ministry team. They even teased us about serving hot chocolate on the streets by asking, "So when are you handing out popcorn and candy too?"

The intersection at Drake and Homer was known as "Boy's Town." The young males were the most receptive to our ministry relative to the other prostitutes. Since they were always hungry, our workers would invite them to the local pizza hang-out. Strong relationships were built and developed. Once they heard the gospel, many of these young men would give their hearts and lives to the Lord Jesus Christ. Other teen prostitutes solicited on Quebec Street and 2nd Avenue.

Scary Moments

As dusk approached, it often felt crazy on the streets. There were so many drug dealers, and people injecting themselves right on the sidewalks and in the alleys. Numerous individuals suffering from mental disorders, as well as those in varying stages of drunkenness, would pass us by; I even was slapped in the face by someone once. Although I wasn't hurt, I sure was stunned.

People have often asked me about the dangers of ministering on the streets. For the most part, it was dangerous but our entire team knew that God was protecting us at all times.

Often the pimps would threaten us, yelling, "Stay away from my woman!" Most times when we spotted them, we did move on because we knew they would take their frustration out on the women, not on us.

Pimps on the West Side each had four to five ladies working for them. Known as "The Family" they sometimes kept the women in check by holding their children hostage. It wasn't safe to work as a renegade prostitute in this area of the city. The pimps sent out enforcers to beat up anyone who attempted to work independently.

My ministry partner, Jack, and I had just started walking up Hastings Street when I spotted a teen I recognized. She was fifteen years old. I had previously known her as "T," the daughter of a neighbor we had in Vancouver. She was about six years old when she became a playmate of my daughters. I was shocked to see "T" working the streets.

As we came closer she felt awkward, embarrassed that I'd found her prostituting. However, as we talked "T" became at ease and asked after my daughters. While we chatted, a rough looking gang of Aboriginals began surrounding us. The angry men were scowling at her. The situation looked ominous. Jack and I knew we were in a threatening situation. We both sent a quick prayer to heaven for protection. "T" also sensed the danger. She glanced over her shoulder and smiled at the scowling young men. Then she promptly turned away from us, said good-bye and walked towards the door of her rooming house. The men followed her silently.

We were left standing alone on the sidewalk; relieved but dismayed at the same time. My heart cried out for her, knowing the potential dangers she was facing. For weeks following that incident I looked for "T" as I passed the rooming house but I never saw her again.

Facing-off With a Pimp

One evening I was talking to a young black woman. Her pimp, a tall muscular mean-eyed guy, approached us and beckoned us to move on. Making eye contact with my ministry partner, I could see he wanted to leave. However, something inside of me rose up and said, "NO WAY!" So, I took a deep breath, and with much boldness from the Lord blurted out, "This is a free country and I can talk to whoever I want!"

My partner looked at me as if I had lost my mind... The seconds that followed felt like hours—my heart was beating anxiously. Did I really say that? What was I thinking? Suddenly, the pimp looked sheepishly at us. He hung his head low and said, "I'm sorry," and then hesitantly asked, "do you have any money for some coffee?" We gave them some hot chocolate. After that, we prayed for both of them.

God continued to create more opportunities for us to minister to pimps. We'd come to the realization that they were just as lost and confused about life as were the prostitutes.

Enchantment

Boy's Town was a 'red-light' district that I was rarely assigned to, however, I had a longing to also minister to male prostitutes. One mid-summer's night, I was given the opportunity to stroll down Drake and Homer. This time, my ministry partner was Jim.

I felt a surge of excitement—something good was about to happen! Sitting on a planter box in front of a worn-out building, a group of ten men congregated around an exquisite young lady. Normally, we wouldn't attempt to approach such a large group. So as a precautionary measure, we stopped and prayed for God's guidance. Within seconds after praying, the woman began to softly sing, "Amazing Grace." I knew this was our cue, so we darted towards them and introduced ourselves.

Zeroing in on Kathy, I told her that she had a beautiful voice. She hung her head low and tried to avoid eye contact. In a quiet, gentle voice she said, "I really love this song." Then she asked, "do you know the rest of the words?" I sat down with the group and sang the entire song to her.

Hastily Kathy scribbled the words on a newspaper she'd found at a nearby bus-stop. After writing all the lyrics, she stepped off the sidewalk on to the road, and stood right in the middle of the intersection. With an astonishingly clear, resounding voice, she sang the full version of "Amazing Grace."

When she finished, I explained what the song was about. Tears filled her eyes. Her face was filled with joy, and her eyes sparkled as we prayed for her. I looked around, and knew that God was present. The young men also had tears in their eyes. Jim and I spoke to them, sharing the good news of the gospel and God's love. There was no resistance from anyone. They gladly listened and accepted the booklets we gave them.

As we departed, I turned around and saw them reading their booklets with Kathy. It had truly been an extraordinary experience. Usually, these young men would not easily talk to us. Another strange phenomenon was that female prostitutes very seldom hung out with their male counterparts.

A week later, on our return, we couldn't find Kathy. We asked the same young men if they knew where she was, and if they'd ever seen her again since that night. They told us that they hadn't. They didn't know who she was or where she'd come from. None of us ever saw her again.

I believe Kathy was sent from God to convict their young tender hearts. They were happy to see us again. The majority of these men became Christians after we shared the gospel with them again. I have a sneaking suspicion that Kathy was one of God's ministering angels.

Heart-Warming Times

Valentine's Day and Mother's Day were special occasions when we would handout flowers and chocolates to the women. At Christmas, we gave away gift bags individually filled with toiletries, candy, shortbread, and a Christmas card including a hand-written note.

The women were thrilled to receive these gifts. Some were more interested in the Christmas card than the gifts because this was the first Christmas card they'd ever received. To this day, it still amazes me how such a small gesture could heal a broken heart and bring about a joyful smile.

A number of the High Track prostitutes had condescending attitudes towards our ministry workers. Often they mocked us or walked away as we approached them. Over the Christmas season, however, the very same women were excited to see our team distributing gift bags. They pursued us like young children eagerly anticipating a special treat. After the holiday festivities, their attitude towards us changed. They became remarkably friendly and more open to talking to us.

It was a sub-zero winter's night close to Christmas when we came across a woman, dressed elegantly in business attire. She was lingering around the Downtown East-side. Appearing strangely out of place, she didn't seem comfortable with her surroundings. As we attempted to greet her, she swiftly walked away from us. We continued to pursue her but she didn't feel like having a conversation. She was so ashamed to be working on the streets. We explained that we weren't here to judge her and only wanted to help.

After chatting for a while, she explained that she was a single mom experiencing financial difficulties—she'd lost her office job due to layoffs. Then she admitted that this was the only way she knew she could rapidly earn some cash to buy Christmas gifts for her kids.

We brought her over to our van loaded with supplies, and gave her a generous bagful of food, candy and gifts. Hugging us tightly to show her deep appreciation, she sighed with relief. Then she promptly gathered up her loot, walked over to the bus stop and took the next bus home.

Chapter 3

Going Deeper

We heartily sang "Happy Birthday" then cheerfully applauded her. Janet's face was gleaming with delight. She felt tremendously loved. Her day hadn't started out that way though.

Just after I woke up that Monday morning, I heard God whisper, "Buy a birthday card." He didn't mention why; I simply knew I had to purchase one to take Downtown for our street ministry that evening. Feeling good about ticking off my to-do list at work, I raced from one task to the next. I didn't feel like going out to the stores, so I brushed off His voice as He reminded me again about the card in the afternoon.

That night we encountered a young woman, weeping incessantly, sitting crouched on the sidewalk. We discovered it was her birthday. No one from her family or among her friends had called with birthday wishes. She had not she received any cards or gifts from anyone she knew either. As she explained the reasons for her tears, I felt the weight of my blunder. It weighed heavily on my mind. The card was for her—God had heard the cries of her lonely heart!

I hadn't obeyed the Lord's prompting that day but He still came to the rescue. Our ministry team was able to take her out for some pop, burger and fries at a nearby restaurant, and that's where we gathered to celebrate her birthday.

From that day onwards, I would check-in daily with the Lord to ask if there was something specific He wanted me to do in regards to my ministry. I'd learnt a tough lesson about the importance of listening to His still small voice.

During the time I served at Crossfire Ministries, I met many outstanding women who were trapped in prostitution for a diversity of reasons. Some were born into prostitution—they had little optimism for a different life or a brighter future.

Not all my encounters were successful. Some ladies, who were acquainted with us, were suspicious of our motives. Several had lost hope, hardening their hearts to God's love. Through God's mercy, however, many were able to break free from the bondage of prostitution, drugs and alcohol and other sinful pursuits.

The biggest stumbling block I had to overcome was my fear of rejection. The "red-light" zones were their territory, and I always felt like an intruder. However, as time passed, I realized that if I spoke lovingly and compassionately, most of the women did want to talk to someone who cared about them.

"Welcome"

I'd been voluntarily ministering to these women for about a year when the realization came that chit-chatting with them on the streets on Monday nights, wasn't enough. As I prayed about this issue, the Lord subsequently gave me some insight on how I could get to know them better and build deeper, more meaningful relationships.

In 1990, an outreach worker from Youth with a Mission introduced me to two stunningly beautiful women. Camille and Coral could've been runway models, gracing the covers of top international fashion magazines. They had recently made Jesus their Lord and Savior, and had turned away from prostitution. The YWAM worker was moving to another city. She was elated that I was willing to disciple them, as they deeply desired to know God more and live for Him.

Camille, Coral and I had a long discussion about their experiences in prostitution and their family lives. I shared my yearning to pioneer a support group for women wanting to leave prostitution. I also wanted to empower them to find an alternate means of income.

Both Coral and Camille were encouraged by the idea and were eager to participate. At our follow-up meeting, we decided to call the group "Welcome." Following that, our next step was to steadily create a support structure.

Life Journeys and Reflections

Over several years, little by little, I was made aware of the life stories of Camille, Coral and the numerous other women who attended our support group. We met once a week in the basement of a church in central Vancouver. Women came from the High Track and the Low Track. Some ladies had worked at escort agencies throughout the city, and some were call girls who had solicited from their homes.

Those who earnestly desired to leave prostitution would go on to experience miraculous changes in their lives. The stories of the women featured in this book, are taken from my encounters and involvement with them. They are not complete stories but recollections from their past lives, as well as glimpses of their lives once I became a friend and mentor to them.

Having received permission from each of them, I will be sharing some of their stories. To protect their identities, fictitious names have been given to all individuals mentioned.

If you are currently working among prostitutes, drug addicts and other vulnerable sectors of society or are thinking of doing so in future, I hope you will be inspired and refreshed by each story.

May your passion to make Jesus known increase! Our magnificent and powerful Lord is able to supernaturally turn around the lives of those making a living on the streets. And to any readers who may be feeling trapped and hopeless, God can give you a renewed purpose in life and a better future as you keep seeking Him.

Chapter 4

Camille

"You're useless! You'll just be a hooker some day!" He vented. In his annoyance, Camille's stepfather often made these cruel remarks to her during her teen years. These hurtful words pierced like a dagger. There was no basis for them. Camille wasn't dating boys and she certainly wasn't dressing inappropriately. Most of her time was spent with her church community—she regularly attended Sunday services and all the youth functions.

Camille grew up with a mom, step dad, an older stepbrother and a younger sister. On the surface, it seemed they were a happy, close-knit Christian family. They were well respected at church and within their social circles. However, things weren't as they appeared.

At home, Camille's fifteen year-old stepbrother was preying on her and her little sister. The sexual abuse began when she was eight, and it continued into her early teens. A few years after the abuse started, she plucked up the courage to tell her mother. Her mom refused to believe any of her allegations; Camille was left abandoned to the advances of her fearsome stepbrother.

In addition, her stepfather despised her and her sister. His constant belittling and humiliation eventually took its toll. Any self-confidence she once had was completely ruined. Feeling alone and abandoned, Camille left home at the age of nineteen.

As a slender, elegant woman with the features of an L'Oreal Paris model, men were attracted to her. She had a perfectly oval face, with an ivory silk complexion and large brown eyes with long, luscious lashes. Her beautiful flowing black hair cascaded down her shoulders. She was searching for love, friendship and acceptance but her male friends were just looking for casual sex.

Camille was young and naïve. She hadn't previously had the opportunity to make choices for herself. Feeling insecure and unprepared for adulthood, she found herself trying it all, alcohol, drugs, sexual promiscuity and wild parties. In due course, she met and fell deeply in love with "Prince Charming." He was her hero — the one man she could depend on to fulfill her dreams.

After a few months of blissful romance and a lavish lifestyle, he told her that he was running low on cash, and suggested that she was sitting on a gold mine. She could work as an elite prostitute, and he would take care of her. Together they could make "big" money, travel the world and settle down together. Camille was totally conned by his plea, "If you love me, you'll do this for me..." His strategy was to gain full control of her by having her fall in love with him, and become completely codependent. This is how most pimps draw in young women.

It took Camille a while to realize she was trapped in a living nightmare. Her dream man had become her captor, her pimp. She managed to leave him by paying him off with money she had earned. By this time, even though she'd left him, she was so accustomed to the sizeable income, the comforts and opulence that she stayed in the game. Besides, her stepfather had always said she'd just become a "hooker" someday.

For a couple of years she worked with other pimps for her own protection. Eventually, she became a renegade. Working on her own she no longer had to split her earnings. Nevertheless, the glamour of an extravagant life and substantial quantities of cash began to diminish. She became nervous and fearful. Detesting what she did for a living, she could barely work. Her self-esteem was lost. Camille hated herself.

To calm her nerves, she began to drink heavily. Ultimately, she came to a point where she could no longer solicit unless she was drunk. Her heavy consumption of alcohol caused her to have many black outs. She couldn't remember how she ended up in various cities, in strange hotels with strange men.

This extremely destructive lifestyle was having a negative effect on both her physical and emotional being; she wanted out. She longed for a 'normal' life but it wasn't going to be an easy path. Could she ever hold a legitimate occupation? Having been out of mainstream society for so long, the adjustment seemed impossible.

However, after some serious contemplation, Camille sought a psychologist to straighten out her life. With the therapist's encouragement, she acquired an entry level day job and upgraded her education at night school. Graduating from a secretarial course, she was employed with a small marketing company.

Comfortable with her new life, Camille began to feel she was finally a part of normal society but she still felt empty inside. Something was bothering her—she had never dealt with her sins and her relationship with God.

She started searching for God. Reading the Bible didn't make her feel any closer to Him. "Is there a God? Does He really care about me?" She wondered. Then one day, it was as though the words leapt off the page in the Bible, *"Then you will call upon me and come and pray to me, and I will listen to you. You will seek me and find me when you seek me with all your heart. I will be found by you," declares the Lord (Jeremiah 29:12-14)*. "Show me the way God," Camille whispered.

God faithfully answered her prayer. A short while later, a young woman from YWAM met Camille and invited her to church. A group of street youth was speaking that day. Her heart was touched; she cried as she heard testimonies of how God had given them homes and changed their lives. She knew that he had brought her here to hear their stories. That day, Camille turned her life over to God and chose to accept Jesus as her Lord and Savior.

She realized that God loved her. Her sins were forgiven. His love and acceptance was unconditional — this was what she'd been looking for all her life.

Shortly after she became a Christian, I was introduced to Camille by the YWAM outreach worker. I was impressed by Camille's story and her desire to help other women who'd given up prostitution. Her friend, Coral, joined us in prayer seeking the Lord as to how we could reach other women trapped in this lifestyle.

Not long after, we launched a support group for ex-prostitutes. Some women who were still active in prostitution also came. Camille and Coral were excited about being part of this group. They contacted several of their friends and invited them to join. Little did they know that the group would become a healing place for them as well as for many others?

Picnic in the Park

It was a beautiful sunny day we were lounging around on the grass watching all the activity. Camille and Coral were intensely watching a family with three teens. This family was having a great time water skiing, and swimming. I observed sadness in Camille and Coral's faces. I leaned over and asked them what was wrong; Camille said they both felt sad because that they missed out on family fun and picnics. There was a great longing in Camille's heart to have a caring loving family. She longed for the approval of a father but all she got was a step father who constantly put her down.

The Downward Spiral

Camille's need for love lead her into dating many unsuitable men who were only interested in short term relationship that included partying, alcohol and sex. Her party life spiraled into binge drinking on the weekends. Many Monday mornings she was so hung over she was not able to work. I was always amazed that her employer didn't catch on to her being absent almost every Monday.

I felt that I had to speak into her life and challenge her regarding her drinking and the men she was hanging out with. It is always risky confronting people with their sin or habits, I knew that she may never contact me again but for her sake I had to take the risk. There was no easy way to confront her so I bluntly said Camille "drinking is destroying your life, self-esteem and your relationship with the Lord, it will rob you of your job, car and everything you have worked so hard to achieve; you need to stop drinking and seek professional help." Camille was so angry with me; she yelled at me "it is none of your blank, blank, business." After I hung up the phone I thought to myself "well that didn't go over very well; so I prayed and asked the Lord to speak to her heart."

A week later Camille called me, she said; "I couldn't believe that you would tell me to stop drinking, how you dare speak to me in that way; but after I cooled down I realized even though it hurt me, I needed to hear the plain truth about my drinking habit." Camille apologized for her harsh words, and asked me to forgive her. After praying with her she realized that she had to come to terms with alcoholism and enter a treatment center.

A New Path

Camille would have to take time off work, this could potentially be a problem because she did not want her employer know she was going to a treatment center. Together we prayed that the Lord would open a way for her to take time off her job for her recovery, God answered our prayers; Camille's employer willingly granted her leave of absence. We both know that this was God moving in her life, within a month she entered a treatment center. After two months in treatment Camille made a strong commitment to the Lord to stay off alcohol, Camille never broke that commitment.

Camille was now on God's path; she attended church, she excelled in her job and she was counseling others in our support group. Camille was a great blessing to the support group because she fully understood how hard it was to change the direction of your life but she also knew the rewards of that change.

Camille became very successful in her job and was respected by her employer and coworkers. On one occasion she was put in charge of setting up a conference for her company. This was a big challenge but the Lord was with her and blessed her work. At the end of the conference her employer had her stand up to receive a standing ovation for a job well done. Camille called me from the conference. She was so excited she said "Bernice now I know what it is like to have self-esteem and confidence I am so grateful for what the Lord is doing in my life."

Camille's life changed from one that was destructive to a life that glorifies God. She is married to a wonderful man. She has four beautiful children and she is a leader in a woman's Bible study in her church.

My journey With Camille has been delightful; I have walked with her through troubling times, and enjoyable times. Over a five year period from the beginning of her recovery to the time she got married we have laughed together and wept together. It has been such a privilege to witness Camille's growth in the Lord. It has been over 18 years since we first met and we still stay in touch as friends sharing with each other the great things God is doing in our lives.

Coral - Walls of Resistance

My first encounter with Coral was during my meeting with Camille. I watched her as she entered the restaurant. I almost felt intimidated by this striking beautiful black woman; she was tall, slender with beautiful long black curly hair, gorgeous large brown eyes and a wonderful deep low soft voice. As we were introduced, I felt her appraising me with her eyes, I could almost hear her say,

"Can I trust this woman?" I knew that she was not going to be won over easily. I smiled at her as we were introduced. The young woman from YWAM spoke for about fifteen minutes. Then Coral started to interrogate me. She asked me; why are you interested in ministering to prostitutes, how long have you been involved with Crossfire Ministries, and what are your qualifications?" As I answered her questions and shared my heart for prostitutes I could see her walls of resistance come down. I could sense that trust was a big issue with Coral but as time went on we built a relationship of love, trust and respect.

Coral was twenty when I first met her; she showed signs of a hard life, even though she was beautiful and appeared confident she was very insecure regarding her capabilities. Due to a lack of parenting she did not have a foundation to discern right and wrong. Throughout her childhood she always felt unwanted, sad, lonely and afraid. Her parents were heavy drinkers and there was a lot of fighting and conflict in Coral's home. One of Coral's fears was loneliness; she told me that she spent many nights curled up in the back seat of her parent's car while they were in the pub drinking.

Her family life had a negative effect on her education. Coral told me that there was no one to get her up to attend school, no one to get breakfast, or to see that she was dressed. Coral often skipped school; as a result she got behind in her grades.

In her early teens Coral started smoking pot and hanging around with a gang of young men who were looking for trouble. They all took great pride in stealing money, and jewelry, for cocaine. The combination of drinking, drugs, stealing, and partying was the only way she knew to cover up her pain.

From the Frying Pan into the Fire

Coral's life at home became unbearable and at the age of fifteen she left home and moved to San Francisco. Shortly after she left home her life spiraled down from stealing drugs to prostitution. Within this time she met an older man who brainwashed her into believing that every woman should be a whore and have a pimp to protect her. He would handle the finer detail of the business of prostitution such as paying for housing, food, drinks, drugs, and clothes. All she had to do was to bring in the money and hand it over to him. She even felt it was acceptable to get slapped around by this man. Coral told me he would beat her up whenever he was irritated. Physical abuse seemed to be paramount in their relationship especially if they were short of money; or if he caught her in the local strip bar instead of working.

Dead-end Street

Fear and excitement often blended together, it was like a drug, but as Coral grew older she began to realize that her life in prostitution was heading down a slippery hill on a dead end street. She would work every night enduring the freezing cold, rain, and constant harassment from the police. People would throw pennies at her and call her a slut. Religious people would drive by and yell out of their car windows "you are sinning and you will go to hell". She had been beaten and raped many times. Coral was desperately trying to keep some shred of dignity but it was fading away quickly.

Coral and her pimp swallowed up thousands of dollars by living in hotels, expensive apartments and spending money on cocaine, alcohol, and many other types of drugs. They were always broke; there was never enough money to pay the rent. Coral found herself working constantly to keep up the demand for money and drugs.

After working in the sex trade for six years Coral began to realize there had to be more to life than working in prostitution, and getting high on drugs. She knew that there was a woman inside of her that was worth more money than any man could pay for. Another deciding factor was that Coral had become pregnant and as a result found it was time to re-evaluate her life. Her pregnancy gave her the determination she needed to walk away from prostitution.

The Transition

Life had always been difficult for Coral and she knew it would be hard to make that transition into the mainstream of society. She recognized that it would take miracle to start a new life. For the first time Coral cried out to God for help. God heard her hearts cry and within a short time Coral met a young woman named Sue, from YWAM. Sue invited Coral and Camille to a youth meeting at her church. I love how God answered Coral's prayer.

"Ask, and it will be given to you; seek, and you will find; knock and it will be opened to you" (Matthew 7:7).

Coral's encounter with God was life changing; she realized money couldn't fill her heart with love and security; only God's love brings forgiveness, fulfillment and security.

Coral was so excited about our Welcome group that she called many of her friends and encouraged them to attend. It was such a joy to watch Coral gently counseling and encouraging the women in the group. During one of our meetings Coral asked us to pray for her, we gathered around her and prayed over every area of pain and sin. As she sobbed deep gut wrenching sobs she experienced God's presence and love touching her and healing her from all the loneliness and pain of her childhood and from the effects of prostitution. God in his infinite love and mercy delivered Coral from the past and gave her hope, and a new life.

One Step Forward, Two Steps Back

With God on her side, the hard work of starting a new life was now possible. Coral knew that she would have to go back to school in order to get a decent job. But first of all she needed to get some work; she managed to acquire a part time job as she upgraded her education.

This new life was much more difficult than she first envisioned. The routine of her job, school and taking care of her baby, was getting her down and to top it off she was always broke.

It wasn't long before depression set in and she started drinking heavily and going to parties. The parting and drinking started to affect her job and school. She knew that she needed to get control of this part of her life if she was ever going to make her goal so she decided to give up the parties but not the drinking.

Being a single mother was another challenge. Coral had no parenting foundation to draw from but in spite of her shortcomings she became a wonderful mother. Coral lived in a basement suite. It was not the best place because her neighbors upstairs were the parting kind that freely smoked marijuana. After visiting Coral's home for a Bible study the smell of marijuana lingered on my clothes. The effect of marijuana smoke made me feel a little hazy.

During one of my visits with Coral I found her very depressed and discouraged. She banged her fist on the floor and cried out, "all I will ever be good for is prostitution." I then realized that the pressure that she was under was leading her back to old thoughts of defeat. We prayed together and worked out some of the problems. My heart ached for her because this was a lonely path and she didn't have the family support she needed. I knew that I would have to be that family to get her through these trying times. We met at least once a week and we were on the phone several times during the week.

The Abuser

When Coral became involved with a Joe, at first he was kind and caring but unbeknownst to her this man had suffered a great deal of abuse in his life and unfortunately became an abuser.

During a friends party Joe and Coral became very drunk. They began to argue Joe became angry and beat Coral so severely that she ended up in the hospital. Coral called me from the hospital. She was crying as she told me about the events of the evening. She said, "Bernice I am so devastated I can't believe he would treat me in such a violent way."

Coral asked if I would take care of her little daughter while she was recovering from the beating. My family was in full agreement with bringing this little one into our home. My teenage daughters were thrilled to have a toddler to play with. During the three days she stayed in our home she watched the Little Mermaid video at least ten times, she could sing all the songs off by heart. What a wonderful blessing it was to have this child in our home. Through this situation my family whole heartily embraced Coral and her daughter.

Following this incident Coral made a decision to enter an alcohol treatment center. When she completed her time at the treatment center she decided to change her career and become a counselor for battered women. Eventually she got a job counseling abused women. She has worked in a facility in the skid row area of Vancouver for over fifteen years. Coral has also become spokesperson for abused women in the Lower Mainland.

Reaching Out

Coral asked me if she could join me on one of my Monday nights on the street. I knew that this would be a big step for her, but I agreed. When we arrived at our designated spot she said "Bernice I don't think I can do this, it is too much of a reminder of my past life." I assured her that she would be okay. Coral's fear melted always as she saw me ministered love and compassion to the women. Coral shared her story how God delivered her from prostitution, drugs, and alcohol. I believe it was at this time God planted the thought in her heart to minister to the women in the downtown east-side.

Coral and Joe re-established their friendship, but it was under the condition that he would seek counseling, which he did. Through counseling Joe recognized the cause for his anger and abuse. Joe became the caring kind man God had meant him to be. Coral, her daughter, and Joe attended church together and over the years Joe became a good friend to Coral and her daughter.

Coral has grown as a person with confidence, courage and compassion. She is an excellent mother. There were many times when she called me for parenting advice. Together we have built the foundation she needed to raise her daughter. Today Coral's daughter is bright a young woman who is intelligent, witty, and a real delight to her mother

Over the past few years Coral explored other faiths but I am confident that she will one day find her way back to Jesus. Coral has not forgotten that it was the Lord Jesus Christ who delivered her from a life of destruction.

I count it as a privilege to have met Camille and Coral, they were both instrumental in teaching me how to relate to women trapped in prostitution. As I ministered Jesus' love to Camille and Coral they in turn encouraged me to press beyond my natural abilities and allow the Holy Spirit to teach me His love and compassion for these dear women.

For He says to Moses, "I will have mercy on whomever I will have mercy, and I will have compassion on whomever I will have compassion." (Romans 9:15)

❄

Chapter 5

God Intervenes

I always find it fascinating how the Lord sets up situations to intervene in our lives. Jenny's friend saw a Crossfire Ministry brochure at the church she was attending. Her friend showed it to Jenny and encouraged her to call Crossfire's office. When I received Jenny's call she sounded apprehensive and very vulnerable. She was very cautious and did not want to give me any information about her life. As I explained to her the purpose of the ministry I could hear a change in her voice, she became more trusting and willing to tell me a little of her life story. I invited her to the Welcome support group. Jenny hesitated and did not want to fully commit to attending. After a lot of encouragement from her friend and her partner Jay she finally came to the group.

Welcome Support Group

The first night Jenny walked into the room, I was awe-struck by this beautiful, tall, slim, First Nation woman with long black hair and piercing brown eyes. Jenny was very quiet and nervous; she was not used to trusting people with her pain, but when she realized all the women in our group had a common bond with her, she relaxed and entered into the discussions. Her walls of protection slowly came down as she shared her story. Jenny was thirty three years old and the mother of three children; her partner Jay was the father of two of the children.

Lost Opportunities

With a lot of regret Jenny told us about her past. Jenny's life started out with great optimism, she wanted a career in Native Justice. While she was in her second year at the University of Saskatchewan she started using drugs. Unfortunately she left university and used prostitution as a way to feed her drug habit. The disappointment she felt was immense; she knew she had blown her career in Native Justice.

After she left university she became pregnant. Jenny's life was becoming more complicated; she was now a single mother hooked on Cocaine, lonely, and desperate.

Jay and Jenny

Jenny and Jay lived together for several years, they had two children. Jay was not working and got into a life of crime; he ended up in jail for two years. When Jay got out of jail he began to attend church, God touched his heart and he received Jesus as his Saviour. He was concerned about the damage prostitution and drug addiction was doing to Jenny and their family: he insisted that she give up prostitution. Jenny was resistant because she did not trust Jay's new found faith. Jenny's lack of trust was due to her family's experience in the Catholic residential schools. In spite of all her disillusionments she still believed that there was a God. However she was very cautious in regards to religion.

New Direction

The Welcome group gave Jenny courage to step into a new direction that was free from drugs, prostitution and shame. As we shared the gospel with Jenny it opened her eyes to the fact that reconciliation with God was possible. Jenny committed her life to Jesus Christ. *"Show me Your way, O Lord. Teach me Your paths, lead me in Your truth and teach me, for You are the God of my salvation, on you I wait all day." (Psalms 25,4-5)*

Welfare was not enough to take care of their family but God intervened by connecting Jay with a Christian man. This man found Jay a job and encouraged him to attend AA meetings. For the first time in their relationship, both Jenny and Jay were off drugs, attending AA meetings and going to church. There was a remarkable change to their family life; the house was clean, the children were cared for and there was food in the cupboard.

Relapse

Jenny's first relapse was for a short period of time. But her second relapse involved both of them. This time the consequence of relapsing was devastating; their children were removed from their home. Both Jenny and Jay ended up in separate treatment centers. When they got out of the treatment center Jenny vowed that she would never use drugs again and she would never put her children in jeopardy. Once they completed their recovery, they were allowed to have their children back.

Reaching out to First Nations Youth

As a result of their relapse and time in recovery Jenny and Jay decided to take a substance abuse counseling course. Their goal was to reaching First Nation Youth who were trapped in addictions. Jay got a job working in an Aboriginal youth center. Jenny continued to take courses that would lead her into a career working with native youth.

The Big Day

Jenny and Jay had been living together for several years and now they had four children. They both knew that they were soul mates and it was time to get married.

I will never forget the day of their wedding. It was a beautiful warm sunny day. The ceremony was held in a local park. The groom stood under a big tree looking very uncomfortable and nervous. Jenny and her maid of honor walked along a path that went around some shrubbery, trees and then over a small bridge which ended up where Jay was standing. Jenny wore a beautiful white dress with a tiara made of a sage branch. Sharing their first kiss as a married couple looked precarious, Jay had to keep his distance to avoid being scratched by the tiara. To signify their oneness a large blanket was wrapped around both of them. Their reception room was filled with hope and joy; it was a true testimony of God's redeeming grace.

Hope Deferred

While Jay was working, Jenny was upgrading her job skills. It appeared that they were a happy family. But the enemy of our soul is never too far away and temptation once again disrupted their lives. Over the course of their marriage Jenny found herself outgrowing her dependence on Jay.

Instead of attending church Jay began to attend a lot of AA and NA meetings. As a result Jay started to pull away from Jenny and the children. The NA and AA meeting became a place where Jay met a lot of young attractive women; his interest in helping these women was not going over too well with Jenny, she finally confronted him about his motives.

There were other difficult issues in their marriage. There was conflict between Jenny's oldest daughter and Jay. Jenny found herself refereeing between them almost every day. Their marriage relationship was definitely going down hill. The final straw for Jenny was when Jay stared to use crack cocaine. Jenny gave Jay the option to go back to the treatment center or leave their home; unfortunately Jay chose the drugs over his family. *"Hope deferred makes the heart sick; but when the desire cometh it is a tree of life".* (Proverbs 13,12)

Forgiveness and Healing

Jenny tried to resolve their marriage issues but Jay's drug use was out of control. Several years ago Jay was close to death after he had overdosed on crystal methadone; Jenny took him back into her home with the condition that he enter a treatment center, get a job and stay off drugs. Jenny has had to set up boundaries around their relationship in order to protect her and the children. I am happy to say that Jay has been clean and sober for the past ten years. He is working as plumber and he is training his oldest son in the plumbing trade. Jenny's faith in God and her determination to care for her family has been outstanding.

With the Lord by her side Jenny did not buckle under the pressure of her husband's struggle with drugs. Through perseverance and a lot of prayer Jenny is now a Supervisor, Substance Abuse Counselor and Reflexologist at an Aboriginal youth center. She is greatly respected by her peers and the native youth she works with. I believe our Heavenly Father has taken care of Jenny and her family throughout all the trying years. I sense that Jenny, Jay and their children are destined for great things in the future. There is so much more to this woman's heroic story that it would take a whole book to discover how Jenny has been reborn and has reclaimed her native culture and traditions.

Observing Jenny's faith, courage, strength and wisdom, has encouraged me in my own walk with Jesus. *"Be of good courage, and He shall strengthen your heart, All you who hope in the Lord." (Psalm 31, 24)*

Barbara - Welcome Group

While Barbara was visiting her brother in Vancouver she shared with him her struggles with the guilt and shame of her past. Fortunately, Barbara's brother did not dismiss her cry for help; he contacted Crossfire Ministries" office for advice. I told him about the support group for ex-prostitutes. He then relayed the information on to Barbara. Before Barbara attended the group we had a long conversation regarding the integrity of the support group. Because

Barbara was now married she was very hesitant to join the group and share her personal life with strangers. I assured her that all the women in the group had gone through similar circumstances.

When Barbara walked into the room my heart immediately went out to her, the sad look in her eyes was unmistakable. I thought to myself, "what would cause this very attractive twenty nine years old Métis woman to appear so sad?" Barbara had very delicate features; she was tall, and slender, with beautiful long black hair. She glanced nervously around the room; I walked over to her and introduced her to the women in the room. After a few introductions she started to relax and actually smiled.

Part of the welcome program was to share a summary of our life's story. As each woman shared their story I could see tears in Barbara's eyes. Even though Barbara had been out of prostitution for some time the shameful effects of her past life were still haunting her. Much to my surprise Barbara overcame her fear; and she plunged right into her life's story. She said, "this is the first time I have felt safe enough to talk about my past." Words of guilt and shame tumbled out of her mouth for over thirty minutes. The other women in the group, with tears in their eyes, patiently sat and listened to her. At the end of her story the women gathered around her and prayed God's healing over her. After many deep sobs and tears Barbara was set free from the power of darkness and condemnation. She walked out of that meeting a new woman. She told us that a great weight had been lifted off of her; she felt loved, encouraged and set free. I was amazed to witness the level of love and compassion the women in our group had for each other.

The Mask

Barbara's mother had seven children; she was a prostitute and a drug addict. When Barbara was six years old all the children were removed from the home, never to see each other for years.

Shortly after the children were removed Barbara's mother died of a drug overdose. The pain of losing her family was etched deep into Barbara's young mind. She vowed that when she had children she would not abandon them. After her mother died Barbara's childhood was very unstable; she was in and out of foster homes therefore she did not have any security in her young life. Barbara was physically and sexually abused many times. She didn't know who she was or who she belonged to. Her only way of coping was to wear a mask to hide her feelings and pain. This mask became her security. "This is typical of children who are abused".

Strings Attached

When Barbara was a teenager she met a man who lavished her with extravagant gifts; she was very impressed and totally take in by his attention but she did not realize there were strings attached to the gifts and it was not long before she became his live-in prostitute. Her pain grew deeper and more intense and she withdrew even deeper within herself. While she was living with this man Barbara gave birth to three little girls. Her home seemed to be just as dysfunctional as the one she lived in with her mother. Barbara reached a point where she needed an escape from the deep pain of being used and abused.

Barbara's partner was a cocaine dealer, and he supplied her with free drugs. He knew that if she was hooked on drugs she would not leave him. The drugs stopped Barbara's pain for a while, but the problem with drugs is that it takes over your body and you can never get enough. When Barbara was cut off from cocaine she suffered physical and mental torment along with guilt. She felt that no one could help her. When she looked into her little girl's faces and big eyes she felt so guilty; they had so much trust and love. She often said to herself, "How can I do this to them?" "What right do I have to put them through this nightmare?" During times of sobriety a haunting memory of her mother came back to her. She would question herself, "was she becoming her mother's daughter?" "Did she want to live and die like her mother?" "Did she want her children to be taken away?" All these questions kept revolving in her thoughts.

The Shift

In desperation Barbara left her partner and moved out on her own with her three little girls. They rented a large old house with an oil furnace, the house was not insulated therefore the house was cold during the winter. During the first winter in this old house they ran out of oil. Barbara went to the welfare office for help, unfortunately they turned her down. The burning question in her mind was how was she going to take care of her three little girls?

With no job skills and poor education she felt that her only option was to work in prostitution. Barbara vowed to herself that she would only work for a short time; she just wanted to get enough money for food and oil…

She was not prepared for the life style of street prostitution. Her first experience was demoralizing; deep down it repulsed her. She remembered crying and feeling like the child she once was when she was first abused. The feelings of being violated were the same, but this time she had consented. After a few months the only way she could cover up the pain of working in prostitution was by using drugs and alcohol.

The big money soon became an addiction, and she couldn't believe she made four times the amount she needed for the rent and oil. Each night as she crossed over the bridge from Surrey toward Vancouver she would become a prostitute. When she returned home and crossed over the bridge to Surrey she reverted back to being a mother to her three little girls. There were times when she was not sure who she was anymore, so she hid behind her mask. She justified her work as a prostitute by thinking she wasn't going to let her kids go without heat again; "I'm doing this for love". But in her heart she felt sadness, loneliness and fear. She hoped and prayed she would meet someone who would love her and accept her – unconditionally.

Deepest Desire

After living in Surrey for several years Barbara decided to give up prostitution and moved back to her hometown. Shortly after she moved she started attending church, it was here she met Jesus Christ and turned her life over to Him. At last her deepest desire was met; Barbara found the only one who would accept her unconditionally. Her struggle with drugs and alcohol was next on her list, she prayed and asked Jesus to give her the strength to quit. Within a short period of time her craving for drugs was gone. Now she was really free from her destructive and sinful life. Finances were still a problem but with the Lord's strength she was able to fight the temptation of returning to prostitution.

While attending church Barbara met a wonderful Christian man, they got married and added a son to their family. Barbara could not fully enjoy her new life because she had not told her husband about her past, she had a great fear that he would despise her and leave her. In addition to her dilemma she did not feel that she deserved her husband. She finally got up the courage to tell her husband the whole story. At first he was shocked and felt cheated but after awhile he realized God's healing and mercy in Barbara's life.

Several months later he started to ask Barbara for exotic sexual encounters. Barbara was devastated and once again felt like a prostitute. She was so upset by her husband's reaction that she had to leave her home to sort out her feelings. She decided to visit her brother in Vancouver. She stayed there for about a month and attended the welcome support group. Within this time there was significant healing in Barbara's heart. Barbara's husband also experienced God's loving mercy and forgiveness. He realized that Barbara was a new creation in Christ.

"Therefore if anyone is in Christ he is a new creation; old things have passed away; and all things have become new." (2 Corinthians 5,17)

The Lord has restored to Barbara all that was stolen from her. Today Barbara walks before the Lord with joy, peace, dignity and self-respect. Jesus has changed her life and He will never forsake her or her family. Barbara knows what it is like to be forgiven, healed and set free of sin, sexual abuse, drug and alcohol addiction, and prostitution. God is in the business of reconciliation and restoration lives.

"But now he has reconciled you by Christ's physical body through death to present you holy in his sight, without blemish and free from accusation." (Colossians 1,22)

Chapter 6

June - An appointment with God

Standing in the entrance of the lane on Princess Street, June was curiously watching us handing out hot chocolate. I looked over in her direction but due to the darkness I could not make out her features.

When we walked toward her I saw a woman about thirty years old dressed in a seductive manner with a sweet round face with sad blue eye. She deliberately turned away from us and walked down the alley. It was quite apparent that she did not want to talk to us, but God had an appointment with her.

We continued walking down the alley talking to a number of women. We eventually caught up to June and offered her some hot chocolate. June asked me, "who are you and why we were giving out hot chocolate?"

I told her we were with Crossfire Ministries and our mandate was to help women who worked in the prostitution trade. As we shared God's love to her I could see the hunger in her eyes but there was suspicion and fear in her voice. I could see that June was anxious to get rid of us so I gave her one of the testimony booklets and moved on.

Second Encounter

Several weeks later I saw June in the same place. When I walked up to her, I felt that she was really uncomfortable. She told me to go away; she said, "you are bad for business; you are driving away my customers." I thought to myself, "that is a good thing." I quickly told her about the Welcome group. I made arrangements to pick her up and take her to the meeting. She agreed to attend but I know it was only to get rid of us.

To my amazement June showed up at the appointed meeting place I hardly recognized her because she was dressed in a nice blue skirt, white blouse and her hair was tied back with a white ribbon, she looked lovely. She hardly spoke on the way to the meeting. I could feel her nervousness. When we parked outside the church she was taken back, she said "Oh I didn't know that we were going to church." I assured her that we were using the church as a meeting place and that the Welcome group was the only people in the church.

The women welcomed her but I could see that she was very uncomfortable. While I was sitting next to her I noticed that she was shivering. I thought to myself, "she is not going to stay; she is ready to run". But the women in the group won her over with their kind words and love. June eventually relaxed, and listened to the other women's stories. After a few meetings June began to share parts of her life's story.

Good Intentions

After several months of meeting with the group June decided to leave prostitution, but her good intentions were not strong enough. She needed money and prostitution was the only way she knew to support herself. Every Monday night I would look for June, hoping and praying I would find her. Finally one evening I saw her in the alley behind the Astoria hotel. I came up to her and gave her a big hug. She drew back and said, "Bernice don't you know that's bad for business." I laughed and said, "I am just going to stand here and hug you so no one will pick you up." Then we had a serious talk about her starting a new life. June agreed to make another attempt to give up prostitution and drugs.

Freedom and Joy

June and her partner Jerry lived near Princess Street. He had a small business in the East Hastings area. Jerry was a kind man; he felt that he was protecting June by having her live in his home. As June gradually stepped into her new life, she started to reclaim her lost childhood.

Jerry was concerned that perhaps June was reverting too far back to her childhood, because all she wanted to do was play board games and other childish games. Jerry called me and asked if June was mentally ill. Fortunately this childish period only lasted for a couple of months. Cycling was another area of her life she regained. She loved cycling all over town and around Stanley Park. For the first time in years June was experiencing freedom and joy.

One evening while I was driving June home from the Welcome meeting, she asked me if she could share some dark things from her past. I said yes; not knowing that I was about to hear one of the most disturbing story I have ever heard. Everyone's story was distinctive but June's story was heart wrenching. While I was driving, June started to pour out her story. It was so full of pain and suffering; I could hardly keep my mind on driving. My heart was breaking and I felt tears flowing down my face. I finally had to pull off the road and park the car.

The Street Kid

June was the youngest of five children. When June was thirteen, her mother's boyfriend raped her. June told her mother, but instead of getting support her mother became jealous and angry. She saw her daughter as competition; therefore her mother kicked her out of the home.

June became a street kid and in order to survive, she turned to prostitution. In spite of her situation June was determined to put herself through school. She also attended church where she accepted Jesus as her Saviour.

A Nightmare Marriage

Shortly after June graduated from High School she married Ron and had three children. Ron was a very violent man he often beat June and the children. June ended up in the hospital many times with broken arms, other lacerations, and most of her teeth knocked out She was aware that Ron often committed crimes outside their home. There were times when she would have to wash blood off the outside and inside of Ron's car. She suspected that he had either killed someone or was involved in a hit and run accident. June never dared question Ron about the blood on the car; she learn to play dumb rather have another brutal beating.

Ron was not only brutal with June; he also beat their children, if she interfered he would beat them harder and beat her as well. June tried to run away with the children but Ron found her. He beat her, so viciously that she ended up in a mental institution. Her trauma was so severe that the doctors felt that she would be permanently mentally handicapped.

Human Resources stepped in and removed the children. Shortly after the children were removed from the home Ron was charged with criminal assault and child abuse. Unfortunately June was in such bad shape physically and mentally that she could no longer care for her children. June felt the only way to protect her children from Ron was to give them up for adoption. While Ron was in prison June divorced him and tried to resume some normality in her life.

A Prime Target

June's mental disabilities made her a prime target for manipulative men; she did not seem to have the capacity to discern men's motives.

When she met Eric she had no idea that he was a pimp. Shortly after they got married he forced her to work for him as a prostitute. After several years June was able to escape from Eric, she divorced him and moved out on her own.

June got a job in a nursing home but her job ended when she started to use drugs. Her drug addictions led her into multiple abuses. After listening to her story for over an hour, I was over whelmed with sadness. June wanted to continue on with her story, I quietly prayed, "Lord please give me the compassion and wisdom I need to help this wounded woman.

An Evil Path

June started to shake and cry as she continued on with her story. She told me that she had been invited to a séance: for a lark she decided to attend. Unfortunately, her curiosity took her down a very dark evil path; she became involved in satanic sexual rituals which severely affected her mind and broke her spirit. As I listened to the gruesome details of these rituals I felt sick inside, my head was reeling; I thought I might vomit. I thought to myself how could anyone survive such a life and still be sane. I reached over to June and held her as she wept; I prayed that God would heal her heart, mind and emotions.

The Transition

What a joyful day it was to see this precious woman recommit her life to Jesus Christ and step into the waters of baptism. Shortly after June's baptism her partner Jerry received the Lord. After Christ came into their lives they decided to live apart.

Change came slowly for June, her many traumas, drug use, and prostitution life style made it difficult for her to study, but in spite of her condition she pressed on to upgrade her education with the Job Start program. Unfortunately June's confidence was still too low to even attempt looking for a job.

Out of fear June sabotaged her recovery by turning back to drugs and prostitution. I found it hard to believe that this was June's comfort zone. Her relapse did not last very long she realized that her old comfort zone was a bit of Hell. Out of desperation June called me and asked if she could get into a recovery house. I happily made all the arrangements. While June was in the recovery home she was able to deal with her pain of abandonment, rejection and codependency. Through the loving care of the staff in the recovery home June's faith and self-esteem began to grow.

"God heals the broken hearted and binds up their wounds." (Psalms 147:3)

With God all Things are Possible!

June graduated from the recovery program and moved into a small apartment on Hastings Street. It was here she met Ray, he lived down the hall from June and soon they became good friends. They both attended our Bible study and during this time Ray committed his life to the Lord.

In 1995 June and Ray were married in their friend's back yard. It was a beautiful bright sunny day. The bride wore a lovely pink flowered dress and the groom wore a light grey suit. Throughout the day it felt like Jesus was smiling down on them. The joy in the air was contagious with balloons and streamers everywhere. There was roast pig on a barbecue spit and a variety of food. Our whole ministry team was thrilled to see this couple so happy. The bride and groom spent their honeymoon camping at Alice Lake. Alice Lake was their favorite camping area and they often celebrated their anniversary there.

New Adventures

All the courses June took over the years gave her self-confidence to minister and care for other addicts. June and Ray reached out to addicts in the rooming houses they managed. They are presently assisting with a recovery house in Vancouver. If anyone knows the ups and downs of recovery it is these two people.

I love talking to June; she is so upbeat and excited about what God is doing in her life. I am so proud of June's willingness to overcome many of her demons and insecurities.

Throughout the years that I have known June, I have witnessed God's unlimited love, mercy and patience toward her. The Lord has taken the ashes of June's life and turned it into a thing of beauty. He has healed her broken spirit and given her the spirit of joy. *"To bestow on them a crown of beauty instead of ashes, the oil of gladness instead of mourning and a garment of praise instead of a spirit of despair." (Isaiah 61:3b)* I count it a privilege to be part of this courageous woman's life and witness God's gentle patient love for her.

Ellie "God doesn't Love Prostitutes"

As a way of throwing us off our guard Ellie, confronted us with these cutting words. For over nine months I tried to talk to Ellie but when I tried to approach her she would walk away, she made it very clear she did not want to talk to us. I could tell that she was going to be one tough woman to get to know. One evening while Ellie was standing at the side of the Patricia Hotel, Maureen and I caught her off guard. Ellie didn't move she just looked at us with a belligerent look, as if to say "who do you think you are and what are you doing in my space?"

Ellie was a tall beautiful black woman about twenty three years old with long black curly hair, beautiful smile and an infectious laugh. When we introduced ourselves, she seemed quite resigned to the fact that she finally had to deal with us. We told her that she did not have to be afraid of us and if she didn't want to talk to us we would leave. But much to our surprise she was very friendly and wanted to talk. She asked us what we were doing in the area and we told her we were there to share God's love to women involved in prostitution. She said to us, "God doesn't love prostitutes." I knew that this was one of those God moments.

We shared the story of Jesus rebuking the religious leaders in the temple in *"Assuredly, I say to you that tax collectors and harlots will enter the kingdom of God before you." (Matthew 21:31)* We continued to share that Jesus had come to set the captives free, and through His death on the cross He has made a way for us to be set free from our sin and shame. We asked her if she would like to receive Jesus as her Saviour. Much to our surprise she answered "yes." Right there on the street she asked Jesus to forgive her for her sins and for Him to come into her life. She cried and laughed at the same time. We gave her our phone number and invited her to our Bible study at Jane's place. She seemed very excited about it and promised to attend.

Ellie enjoyed the attention everyone gave her at the Bible study; she was not shy in sharing her life story. Her life was fairly normal until her mother died. Ellie was only twelve years old; she felt that her world had come to a sudden end. Her father tried to look after the children but he was overwhelmed with working and caring for his family. Regrettably the children grow up without guidance.

Looking for Love

Ellie was lost without her mother, she turned to friends for comfort but her so called friends turned her on to drugs and sexual encounters. At the age of fifteen Ellie became pregnant and she gave birth to a baby girl. This was a case of a baby having a baby. She had no idea how to care for this baby therefore the baby ended up in a foster home. Fortunately Ellie was able to visit baby K during the five years that she was in the foster home.

Her Social Service Worker was able to assist Ellie in getting her five year-old daughter back, with the condition that she would move into a group home that cares for single moms and their children. Ellie was really happy about being reunited with her daughter. She wanted to learn how to be a responsible parent. In this group home, Ellie was learning how to cook and take care of her daughter but after several months the novelty wore off; she missed the action on the street. Ellie started to leave her daughter with the other moms in the home. The staff at the group home asked Ellie to leave and baby K went back into foster care. It wasn't long before Ellie was back with her old friends and working in the prostitution trade.

Russian Roulette

Many prostitutes say, "being raped is part of the price one pays; it is a game." The risk can be exhilarating or devastating.

There are no safe customers. Ellie was standing in her usual place soliciting when a van stopped in front of her. The driver opened the door and invited Ellie in. There were four men in the van but Ellie didn't see them because the van hand no side windows. Ellie tried to get out but the driver stepped on the gas and the men restrained her. They drove to Stanley Park and there the four men beat and raped her. Then they drove back to where they picked her up and kicked her out of the van. Ellie managed to call the police and report the incident but there was not much they could do because Ellie did not have the van's license number.

Ellie was so devastated by this experience that she tried to commit suicide. I received a phone call from a nurse at Vancouver General Hospital who told me that Ellie wanted me to visit her. When I arrived at the Psych ward I had to leave my purse at the nurse's station. I was taken to a small room with padded walls, and bare floor, and a mattress. I was shocked to see Ellie curled up on the mattress sobbing. I sat on the floor with her and held her in my arms; she shook all over and cried as she told me about her experience with the men in the van. I felt so helpless; all I could do was comfort her and pray with her. I didn't want to leave her there but I knew that she needed to be there for her own protection.

I was hoping that this experience would discourage her from continuing on in prostitution but a few days after arriving home she was right back in her usual spot soliciting. Her craving for drugs was more important to her than the danger of another rape episode.

Ellie required a lot of support due to all that she had suffered physically, mentally and emotionally. She tried to draw support from every resource she could find; this lead to a great deal of confusion. Our team and the social worker decided to work together; we convinced Ellie to enter a recovery center. Ellie stayed for a few months but she had a difficult time obeying the rules of the center so she decided to leave. Over a two year period Ellie was in and out of recovery centers. Ellie's attitude toward authority and rules was defiant, "they are not going to tell me what to do". This defiant attitude landed her right back down on the street, on drugs, and in prostitution.

Consequences

Infections among intravenous drug users are quite common, especially if they share needles.

One evening while we were ministering in the East Hasting area I saw Ellie leaning against a store front wall, I knew something was wrong because she looked very sick. I called out to her to come into the van. Then we noticed a terrible smell coming from her. I looked at her arm and saw that it was swollen and infected. We took her to the hospital for treatment. Thank God the nurses treated her immediately.

I convinced Ellie to go back to the recovery home but once again she would not cooperate with the staff. When she moved out she met a man; he seemed to be interested in her but their relationship did not last. While she was involved with this man she became pregnant. Her pregnancy caused Ellie to re-evaluate her life style;

she stopped prostitution and using drugs. She was a different person she was full of fun and loved to laugh.

Ellie's twins were born premature; a beautiful boy and a girl. I had the privilege of holding and feeding these beautiful babies in the hospital nursery. Ellie's social worker knew that Ellie was not able to take care of the twins. Within a day after they were born Ellie had to sign the twins over to Social Services. It was very difficult for Ellie to give up her babies but she recognized that she was not mentally or emotionally able to care for them. Ellie bravely signed them over to be adopted with the condition that the twins would not be separated and it would be an open adoption. I was so proud of her for her unselfish decision. Giving up a child is always heart-wrenching for the mother. I found that my own heart was breaking as we cried together, I held Ellie as she sobbed and grieved over the loss of her babies. *"Rejoice with those who rejoice, and weep with those who weep." (Romans 12:15)*

New Attitude

After the babies were born something changed in Ellie's attitude; she agreed to return to the recovery home. She cooperated with the staff even to the point of helping them with other women in the recovery home. She graduated from the program with a strong determination to walk a new path. Ellie attended church regularly and was baptized. The pastor and his wife took her under their wing, loved and cared for her.

Eventually Mental Health arranged for her to live in a semi controlled home where she had her own suite and was monitored daily. Part of the program in this home was art therapy. Ellie soon found out that she had an outlet for some of her pain as well as finding a hidden talent in art. Ellie left the home several times and tried to live with a friend, but this always ended up in failure because they were not able to get along together.

Ellie had been off drugs for approximately two years when she met a man much older than her. He was in his late forties. After several months of courting, they decided to get married. Shortly after their wedding Ellie met a young woman who needed a place to live, she felt sorry for the woman and invited her to live with them. Unfortunately the woman caused a lot of conflict in the home. Ellie's husband started to abuse Ellie; the situation became so bad that she had to flee for her life.

I was so proud of Ellie for the mature way she handled this new crisis. She did not relapse back to her old life style; she was determined to work on her recovery. Ellie contacted her Mental Health worker; they moved her into a center for women who had experienced serious trauma. This center was a God-send for Ellie. I appreciate the love and patience the staff showed toward Ellie creating healing and stability in her life. After Ellie graduated from the trauma center she returned to a semi private home provided by Mental Health Services.

You may be wondering about her children. Her oldest daughter is twenty four and married and the twins are eighteen. The twins still live with their adoptive parents. Ellie has built a good relationship with the adoptive parents. The children visit Ellie several times a year. Ellie's struggle with drugs has been one day at a time. She has been off drugs and out of prostitution for over fourteen years. Praise the Lord!

For twenty years I have walked through many difficult occasions with Ellie. I have seen her fall and get up, I have witnessed her fear, pain, sorrow and joy. God has put many people in His daughter's life to nurture her, but He has been Ellie's ultimate support.

Many people thought that this woman's life was hopeless. Over the years Ellie upgraded her education; she finally got her grade twelve certificate. Nothing is impossible with God; He has a plan and destiny for Ellie.

There was another side to Ellie that always amazed me; it was her concern for other women who were trapped in prostitution. One evening she called me and told me about a young woman named Candy. She was very concerned about Candy and asked me to help her; soon Candy became another young woman I had the privilege to know.

My relationship with Ellie is ongoing; she calls me at least once a month. I often feel that she is checking in with me to make sure I am okay. Ellie attends a church in New Westminster; where she is encouraged and supported to follow the path that God has set before her. Once again, the Lord has proven to me that He is in the business of reconciling people to Himself.

"But now he has reconciled you by Christ's physical body through death to present you holy in his sight, without blemish and free from accusation." (Col 1:22)

He is the potter and we are the clay. *"But now, O LORD You are our Father; we are the clay, and You our Potter; And all we are the work of You hand." (Isaiah 64:8)*

Chapter 7

Candy's Story - Street ballet

I have seen and heard many bizarre spectacles during my ministry on the streets of Vancouver, but this image I will never forget. There was a soft glow in the sky as the sun was setting. I looked across the street and saw a young woman in jeans and a white top performing a ballet dance on the sidewalk outside the Patricia Hotel. In the evening light she looked like some whimsical nymph. Some of the people on the street walked past her laughing, but others simply ignored her. Most of the people in the area were used to all kinds of outlandish behavior. I found out later that her nickname was Twinkle Toes.

I felt compelled to talk to this young woman even though she was high on drugs. Candy was about twenty years old, she was tall and very slender, with straggly blond hair and blue green eyes. I walked up to her and said, "Hi, we are with Crossfire Ministries would you like a cup of hot chocolate?" "She said no," and continued on dancing. Generally, we would have moved on, but we felt we should stay there and pray for her. Finally, she walked over to us and asked if we had any money. I told her, "No. We are here to let you know how much Jesus loves you." She said, "Move on, you are in my way. I need to make some money." I then gave her a testimony booklet and told I would be praying for her. As we continued on our journey along Hastings Street, a young woman came up to us and warned us to be careful around Candy. She said: "watch out for Candy; she is dangerous; she attacks people, and steals their drugs and money."

Candy's violent behavior separated her from the other women who worked as prostitutes. Fortunately, Ellie was not afraid of Candy. Ellie often told me that she was concerned and afraid that Candy would eventually overdose on drugs or be killed by one of her clients.

God's Healing Power

June called Crossfire; she was in a panic because Candy was in her apartment going through withdrawal. June didn't know what to do with her. Pastor Culley and I were asked to look into the situation. When we arrived at June's apartment, we found Candy lying on the couch; she was passing in and out of consciousness. We prayed over Candy asking God to clean out her system from the effects of the drugs. Within an hour, Candy sat up fully conscious. She said, "I don't know what just happened. This is the fastest and most painless withdrawal I have ever experienced." We all recognized that this was a miracle because it usually takes three to five days to withdraw from a mixture of heroin and cocaine.

Candy knew that something powerful had touched her body. She asked us, "Why do I feel so great?" We told her that the power of God was healing her. We continued to pray over her asking God to bring healing to her body and broken spirit. Once again she experienced the Lord touching her deep inside her very soul. Candy looked at Pastor Culley and me in awe. She said "I feel such peace and joy all over me; I can't remember ever feeling like this before." We then shared the gospel message with her and told her that Jesus loved her and wanted to set her free her from the bondage of drugs and prostitution.

Candy was not ready to make a full commitment to Jesus but she was open to starting a new life.

I knew that we had to move her out of the area quickly so I contacted Teen Challenge. A young woman who was working at Teen Challenge agreed to take Candy into Teen Challenge's home for a short period. Crossfire Ministry workers and Teen Challenge staff worked around the clock, day and night caring for Candy.

Looking after someone like Candy was challenging, her moods were up and down, and her language was atrocious. Her eating habits were appalling; all she wanted to eat was junk food. She slept during the day and was awake during the night. She was definitely a diamond in the rough.

Encounter with Jesus

I took Candy to the Easter service at my church; during the service, I noticed that she was captivated with the sermon. Near the end of the sermon Candy started to cry; I leaned over and asked her if she was ready to received Jesus Christ as her Lord and Saviour. She said, "Yes, now I understand why Jesus died on the cross." After I lead her to Jesus, I asked the Pastor to pray with her. From that time on, I saw a dramatic change in her behavior and language. Her willingness to change was refreshing to watch.

I have many great memories of Candy and me visiting parks and beaches. Candy was seeing the world through new eyes; she would run around the park like a child, swinging on the swings, or splashing through the water. Her renewed interest for life was invigorating.

Childhood Devastation

As we spent time together I gained an understanding of Candy's background. Candy came from a fairly normal family who lived in a small town. When Candy was twelve years old her parents went on a vacation and left her with her grandparents. While she was with her grandparents, her grandfather raped her. Candy was devastated; she did not know how to handle the situation so she just hid her pain deep inside of her. From that time on Candy's happy childhood changed, she acted out with bizarre behavior, which was argumentative, aggressive, and defiant. In her early teens she turned to illegal drugs and alcohol.

After Candy completed grade ten, she dropped out of school. She became involved with a young man and became pregnant. At the age of seventeen she gave birth to a beautiful baby boy. The stress of being a mother was too much for Candy. She once again turned to drugs in order to cope with life. Candy realized that her addiction to heroin and being a mother was not working, so she gave full custody of her baby over to the child's father.

Candy moved to Vancouver and within a few weeks was soliciting for drug money. Candy had been working in prostitution for approximately four years when I met her.

Too Young to Die

Candy made arrangements with me to drive her to her Doctor's office; she wanted to get the results of some blood tests. When she came out of the office she looked dazed and upset, she had just learned that she was HIV positive. My heart sunk when I heard the news; I sent a silent pray to Jesus, "please show me how to minister to Candy right now." Tears streamed down her face as she cried out, "Bernice I am only twenty two years old; I am too young to die." I pulled the car over to the side of the road, and took her into my arms and prayed that the Lord would comfort and heal her.

In April 1991 Candy moved from the Teen Challenge home to Homestead (Salvation Army's drug treatment center.) Everyone at Homestead was very kind to Candy. While she was at Homestead, she had the opportunity to attend a Christian youth camp. Candy loved the camp and said that she was finally starting to feel like a healthy young woman again. The difference in Candy's appearance was remarkable. She had put on weight, her face glowed with health and her eyes were bright. She looked like a different woman than the young skinny, sad woman I met eight months prior.

Candy became a celebrity because of her remarkable recovery. All this attention started to affect her. The pressure to perform was too much. After being at Homestead for three months, she was allowed to leave the facility to cash her welfare cheque. The temptation of having money was just too great for Candy; money equaled drugs. The people at Homestead called me to let me know that Candy left their facility. I felt sick inside; this was a young woman that many others and I had poured encouragement and love into. She had meals in my home and my children loved her. Soon after the call, my husband and I headed downtown; we found her on Jackson Street buying drugs. I tried to talk to her but she kept evading me. Finally she saw that I was not going to leave; she walked over to me and yelled at me "I don't want to see you anymore; stay away from me." I knew she was trying to ward me off because we were in the midst of several drug dealers who were not very happy with us witnessing their drug transactions. I quietly told her that if she wanted to come back to Homestead they were willing to take her back. She said she was sorry and ran off down the street.

It was so hard to see Candy revert back to her old life style. I made several attempts to persuade her to return to Homestead but she refused. October 21, 1991 I received a call from D, Candy was at the F. S. Treatment Center. She entered the treatment center with only the clothes on her back. I quickly gathered up some clothes for her and went to the F.S. Treatment center. Candy was happy to see me. She said, "Bernice I am sorry! I did not mean to push you away but I felt so guilty every time I saw you." I was shocked to see how rapidly Candy's physical condition had deteriorated. She was very thin, with sores on her body, infected needle marks on her arms, and her skin was grey because she had not been taking her HIV medicine.

Candy said to me, "Bernice. I don't know if I can go through treatment and withdrawal again". Then she asked me, "If I died while using drugs would I go to heaven?" I told her that she still belonged to Jesus and His mercy endures forever. When we prayed together, Candy showed real repentance. I stayed with her and encouraged her to press through the pain of withdrawal. I visited her often but unfortunately she only stayed at the F.S. Treatment Center for ten days. As soon as she received her welfare cheque she took off back to the streets. It is common for alcoholics and drug addicts to relapse as soon as the welfare cheque arrives.

Five days after Candy left The F.S. center, I received a call from June. Candy was once again at her place very dope sick. I called all the Detox centers but they did not have any beds. I called every place I could think of but because of her appalling behavior in the past they were not willing to take her in. Even the Downtown Hotels were not willing to have her. Candy had burned so many bridges that it was hard to find anyone who would take her. Finally Pastor Ernie Cully was able to find a friend who was willing to see Candy through the detox process. November 9, 1991, Candy went back to the F. S. Center but she only lasted one month. She ended up back on East Hasting Street.

The Devastating Effects of Drug Overdose

The next time I saw Candy was in February 1992. It was a dark night, I was walking along Hasting Street across from the Patricia Hotel when I saw a familiar figure of a woman. I decided to walk across the street for a closer look at her. When I got close to her, I realized this woman was Candy. I hardly recognized her, she looked like an old woman limping and her face was distorted. Candy had suffered from a stroke that affected her left side; the stroke paralyzed her face and left leg. She covered her face with her hands and walked away from me. I called out to her

"Candy." She did her best to get away from me but I continued to pursue her. Again I called out to her, "Candy why are you trying to avoid me?" She said, "I am so ashamed I don't want you to see me in this condition." I told her that I loved her unconditionally and gave her a big hug, we both cried as I prayed for her. Once again she asked me, "Bernice does Jesus still love me?" I told her that He loved her with an everlasting love." I tried to talk her into returning to a treatment center, unfortunately Candy refused.

I lost track of Candy for several months. On October 11, 1992 I met up with her at the United Church Women's Center. She was very sick with a chest cold, a deep cough, and a temperature. I took her to Vancouver General Hospital Emergency where we waited for several hours. I was appalled at the indifferent attitude she received from the nurses. Finally at one a.m., they took Candy into a treatment room; they told me not to wait because she would be there for a while.

The next day Candy called me from the United Church Women's Center she sounded very upset. She said, "Early this morning, I stumbled over Rivera's dead body in the alley. Oh Bernice, that could have been me lying in the alley." This incident shook Candy up to the fact that she needed to get back into a treatment center. I made arrangements with the director of Unity House to admit Candy. Unfortunately, Candy only stayed four days and returned to the streets. One of the reasons why Candy had a difficult time staying off heroin was that she suffered a lot of pain from her HIV condition. Apparently the heroin eased her pain and discomfort.

Staying Connected,

It was difficult to contact Candy because she did not have a phone and she changed her place of residence every couple of months. Once in a while I would see her while I was ministering in the East Hasting area. She would hug me and tell me that she loved me. She often told me that she still believed in Jesus but she knew her life was not pleasing to the Lord.

In October 2002, I was given Candy's address from a fellow worker. I went to visit Candy in her small room in an old rundown hotel. I was astonished at how cozy and tidy her little room was. She had decorated this old room with her art and other interesting pieces of furniture. She was so happy to see me, we both cried a little then caught up on how thing were going in her life. I was amazed that she was looking so healthy considering that she had AIDS. I was glad to hear that she was on medication for her HIV condition. She told me that she had overdosed on a cocktail of drugs and ended up with severe paranoia. The mental health police picked her up and took her to the hospital. She said she never wanted to experience that state of mind again so she cut down on her consumption of heroin. Candy is no longer involved in prostitution but she is selling drugs in order to pay for her drug habit. During my time with Candy, we had a sweet time reading the Bible and praying together.

For years, I had stored some of Candy personal belongings in a small suitcase. She was so surprised that I still had them. Before I left Candy I made arrangements to deliver the suitcase. A week later I returned with the suitcase to her Hotel, unfortunately she was not at home. The Manager of the Hotel allowed me to leave the suitcase in her room. I have not seen Candy since my time with her in the hotel, but she is in my thoughts and prayers.

I know that Candy's life is not a perfect example of a Christian, but she has a heart that is soft toward the Lord, she reads the bible and prays every day. I believe that Jesus' love and mercy toward Candy is unconditional.

"Oh give thanks to the LORD for He is good! For His mercy endures forever." (Psalm 106:1)

The Mirror, By Dee

When life is hard and I give up on me,
I look to the wall and in the mirror,
I see beauty, grace, and a young woman's face.
But a mask is also most defiantly there,
it is happy, sad, dark, and fair.
Underneath is a scared little girl who's scared of life,
Who's scared of the world.
Loneliness, anger, deceit,
and hate is all she sees in her lonely world of fate.
She screams cries and claws to be free,
but this little girl is scared you see.
She tries and tries to find her way out
with a tear streaked face. She pleads and shouts,
Lord, if you can hear this young woman's plea,
help to release her,
set this little girl free into a world of love, beauty.
And grace us like the wall and
the mirror that shows her face.

Sara – Great Hopes and Dreams

Not all the women hanging around the downtown East-side area at night are prostitutes. Therefore I had to be careful in the way I approached each woman. Sara was standing on the corner of Jackson and Hastings Street, she was dressed like a young business woman. As I came close to her she gave me a lovely smile and said, "Hi who are you and what are you doing in this area?" Sara was a cute little blond with blue eyes, around thirty years old, with a lovely smile, inquisitive, and bright. I explained our purpose in being in the area. Her face lit up. She said, "That is great, I am so happy to see there are people who care about the women around here." I asked her if she lived in the area and she said, "Yes I live at the Patricia Hotel." As we continued our conversation, I clued into the fact that she was a prostitute. I gave her one of the testimony booklets and invited her to contact me if she ever needed help. She said, "I am okay but you need to take care of yourself. This is a dangerous area of town."

Whenever our team encountered Sara, she would always ask us how we were and when we left her, she would thank us for our visit. Throughout each visit we encouraged Sara to get out of prostitution. Sara had great hopes and dreams but her reliance on cocaine hindered her from having them fulfilled. I enjoyed my visits with Sara, but afterwards I always felt sad that I was leaving a good friend in an evil place.

Stepping Out of Darkness

August 1992, Sara decided to leave prostitution. Sara approached the Welfare Office to sponsor her in a course for office work; Sara was accepted. Sara moved in with her boyfriend who was in a recovery program. I was not too thrilled with these arrangements but it was Sara's choice. Crossfire Ministries helped move them and gave them some household items. After assisting them with the move, we prayed with them and shared the gospel. A week later, Dave and Sara picked up some furniture from Crossfire's Recovery House. While they were there Sara had an opportunity to meet the house director J.H., she gave Sara a tour of the house. I believe that this encounter played a big part in Sara eventually moving into the house.

Sara found out that living with Dave was a big mistake. Eventually they both relapsed. Consequently, Sara ended up working in prostitution again. Near the end of November 1993, we met Sara standing at the corner of Jackson and Hastings Street; I could tell that she was embarrassed to see us. During our conversation Sara mentioned that she would like to go back to school and take a course in accounting. I reminded her of the program at Crossfire's recovery house and within a short while Sara called me and asked if she could live at the recovery house. This was a big step because Sara was apprehensive about giving up her old way of life. Sara would have to live by the rules of the house plus come under the authority of the house director. Sara was given her own room with a cozy bed, dresser and desk. The house director, was an amazing woman, who had the ability to make the residents in the home feel safe, loved, and secure. For the first time in years, Sara experienced security and love.

A few days after Sara moved into the house another young woman moved in. Within a short period of time these two women became good friends. There were the usual conflicts over household duties, and clothes but most of these situations were very similar to any sibling rivalry.

Christmas Blessings

Sara's first Christmas at the recovery house was full of unexpected blessings. All the women helped the staff prepare the Christmas dinner. Crossfire Ministry workers had the privilege of joining in the Christmas celebration. The women in the house made beautiful gifts for each other and for the staff. The Christmas tree was loaded with gifts for everyone. It was so much fun watching the women open their gifts and scream with glee. Everyone was overwhelmed with all the love and gifts. This was the beginning of many great experiences that Sara encountered while she lived at the recovery house.

Bernice with residents at the Recovery House

In 1994, I became the administrator at the recovery house; I taught the twelve step program and counseled the residents. During our counseling sessions Sara would put on a facade, she wanted me to think that she was okay. I knew that she was struggling with guilt from her past and withdrawal from Cocaine. Eventually Sara was able to open up the hurtful places of her childhood.

The Fatal Shot

One of the most traumatic moments in Sara's life was when she was fifteen years old. Her brother and older sister were having a disagreement. Sara's brother found his father's gun and shot and killed his sister. Sara was in such shock that she could not comprehend that the incident really happened. Sara's father blamed her for not preventing the incident. For years, Sara felt guilty that she was not able to stop her brother from shooting her sister. From her early childhood, Sara never felt loved or accepted by her father; she felt that she could never measure up to his high standards. Sara's relationship with her father deteriorated to the point that she felt left out of the family circle. Hurt, lost, and lonely Sara turned to young men for comfort and love.

Wrong Choices

When Sara was seventeen she became pregnant, her family and local priest pressured her into putting the child up for adoption. The decision to give up her baby boy was devastating and still haunts her today.

Sara was twenty four years old when she got married. Within the first year of her marriage she realized that she had made a big mistake, her husband was an abusive, controlling man with a gambling addiction. Three years later, she left her husband and moved to Vancouver.

When Sara arrived in Vancouver, she worked in a hotel bar in the downtown east-side. It was during this time, she developed friendships with prostitutes and drug dealers. Sara was devastated when her mother died, she felt that this was the last straw; she had nothing to live for. In order to cope with all the pain and discouragement she began to use cocaine. It did not take long before she was trapped in the cycle of drugs and prostitution.

Through the counseling sessions, Sara began to experience relief from the pain of rejection and guilt. One evening while we were having a Bible study Sara invited Jesus into her life. The scripture verse that touched her heart was, *"If we confess our sins, He is faithful*

and just to forgive us our sins and to cleanse us from all unrighteousness."
(1 John 1:9)

While living in the recovery house Sara had to confront her fears, rejection, habits, and addiction. There were several disagreements over her perception that the staff favored one woman more than the others. Her need to be accepted became a trap; she would do deeds of kindness in order to gain love and friendship. This would often backfire and hurt her because people would use her for their own selfish motives. She had a male friend who was supportive but he often used her kindness and insecurity for his own benefits.

Excess Baggage

One Sunday while at church Sara had a remarkable experience. The emphasis of the message was about letting go of all the excess baggage from parents, grandparents and sinful habits. While Sara was praying, she could see in her mind a mist flowing from her body with a bright light behind it. There were images of large objects leaving her. She felt that the Lord had taken great weights off her. I believe the Lord gave Sara this vision to show her that she was now free of the past. After this incident, the house director noticed a change in Sara's attitude; she was more tolerant and compassionate toward the new residents.

Testing Times

While traveling throughout the city, Sara was often confronted by drug dealers. Sara learned to pray for God's protection and strength to help her to resist the temptation that was before her. She prayed, "Lord give me the strength to say no and walk away from these situations." During her early days in recovery she had dreams about using. She would wake up shaking and feel a strong urge to use cocaine. Each time she would cry out to the Lord to deliver her from her addiction. This is a quote from her journal, "I am afraid that if I use cocaine again I will die. I know that I am a sinner but if I keep plugging away and give everything to Jesus My Savior. I know I can overcome everything and walk with Him."

While Sara lived in the recovery house, she held down a part-time job and went back to school to upgrade her education. Sara was a good model for the other residents in the home; they saw how hard she worked on her recovery as well as moving forward in her education. Several of the residents followed Sara's example and upgraded their education. In September 1994, Sara took a course in Business Administration at Kwantlen College. This was a big step but she had a lot of support from all the staff at recovery house. Everyone was very proud of her when she completed her course and graduated with high marks.

By this time Sara had lived at the recovery house for two years; with a degree in her hands Sara was now ready to look for work. It has been my observation that many recovering addicts relapse after they have completed their education or some special goal. The daunting task of applying for work and being rejected is sometimes too overwhelming. In order to avoid this problem. Sara was encouraged to join The Job Club. This short course taught her how to apply for a job and prepare a resume. The staff at the recovery house realized that in order for Sara to present well in an interview, she needed a makeover. The staff collected some money and took Sara shopping for some new clothes and a new hair style. This not only helped Sara's self-esteem but she really looked the part of a professional office worker.

Sara found it very difficult to acquire a job, everywhere she applied the employers wanted at least two years' experience. Crossfire's office contacted several Christian businesses and finally a Christian business man hired Sara. Now that Sara was fully established in her job, she was ready to move out of the recovery home and to find her own place. The staff helped her to find a little apartment and assisted her in her move as well as finding furniture, appliances, and utensils for her. There was a mixed feeling of joy and sadness as everyone said their good-byes.

Shortly after Sara left the recovery house she decided to get baptized. I had the privilege to stand in the baptistery tank with her. What a fantastic experience it was to see her glowing smiling face as she came out of the water.

Sara worked with this Christian company as an assistant accountant for three years. Unfortunately the business failed and her employer could no longer afford staff. Since that time she has had several jobs in accounting but most of her jobs have been part-time. Unfortunately, due to serious health problems she could not work for about a year, therefore she had to go on welfare. After her treatment she was able to return to work as an assistant accountant.

Answered Prayer

One of Sara's prayers was to re-establish her relationship with her family. In 1998 Sara's father, sister and brother from Ontario came to visit her. During their visit her sister and brother apologized for the incidents they had falsely accused Sara of. Sara's father was shocked at their confessions because he always thought that Sara was the trouble maker. This was the turning point in Sara's relationship with her family. God answered Sara's prayers for reconciliation and restoration with her family. Sara completely forgave her sister and brother, and their relationship was restored.

Second Family

Sara considered Crossfire workers, staff, and residents her second family. Because of this relationship Sara wanted to give back by helping others who had fallen into the trap of addictions and prostitution. In addition to her part-time job she decided to volunteer as relief staff at the recovery house. Sara was a great blessing to the staff and residents; she loved cooking for the residents and taking them out to AA meetings, doctor's appointments and shopping.

Sara was very generous; she bought the women in the house gifts for their birthdays and Christmas. Because Sara was a caregiver she often found that she was taken advantage of by the very people she was helping but she knew that this was par for the course. Eventually Sara landed a full time job and had to give up working at the recovery house.

Sara often said to me, "Bernice I really want to have a healthy, loving relationship with a man."

In the past she often made poor choices in male relationships. We both prayed that the Lord would arrange for Sara meet a nice gentleman. I am happy to say that Sara has found a wonderful man; they have been friends for the past nine years.

Throughout the years Sara and I have remained friends, I love getting together with her for coffee or lunch. I am always inspired by this bright joyful women, I believe that her faith in God has carried her through many hard situations. I believe that this verse describes Sara's heart

"I know what it is to be in need, and I know what is to have plenty. I have learned the secret of being content in any and every situation, whether well fed or hungry, whether living in plenty or in want. I can do all things through Christ who gives me strength." (Philippians 4:12-13)

Chapter 8

Oliana – The Hawaiian Beauty

Ministering in the high track area of Richards Street was always an intimidating experience. The prostitutes in this area were always dolled up with expensive outfits, spiked heels and an air of superiority. I wore jeans, sports shoes and a big yellow jacket, carrying a pump thermos of hot chocolate; it was a huge contrast. As we were walking along offering hot chocolate to the women we encountered a beautiful young woman. Her features were similar to the beautiful women that would greet you as you got off the air plane in Hawaii. She had exotic features with an oval face, long black hair and large brown eyes. Oliana would always acknowledge us and take a testimony booklet but like many of the other women she did not engage in any serious conversation. She told us that she was okay with her life style and did not need our help or the gospel message. Oliana gave us many excuses for the work she was doing, I had heard many women give these excuses. I knew that this was their way to justify their actions.

The Call

I was not surprised when I received a call from Crossfire's office that Oliana needed help. She had fled from her pimp and was in hiding at a friend's place but this place was no longer safe. Oliana was terrified that her pimp had sent out his enforcer to find her and bring her back. Oliana feared for her life because this man brutally beat up other women who tried to leave prostitution. This was a crisis that had to be attended to, quickly. We called several women's centers and churches and finally found a Christian home that had just opened a safe house for abused women.

Clifford and I arranged to meet Oliana and her uncle at a restaurant in Vancouver. Her uncle was a retired policeman. He wanted to check us out before he handed Oliana over to our care. When I walked into the restaurant I looked around for Oliana. At first I could not see her, but then I looked over to a booth and saw a young woman with an older man. She was dressed in a sweat shirt, her hair was messy, and she had dark circles under her eyes. She looked like a freighted little girl huddled there in the corner of the booth. What a difference from the confident woman I saw on the street who said "I am just fine". She recognized us and gave us a wave and a half smile. Then she introduced us to her uncle. Oliana's uncle asked us a lot of questions about the ministry and the safe house. We exchanged phone numbers and other essential information, he was then satisfied that we would take care of his niece. We concluded our conversation and left the restaurant. I could see the concern in her uncle's eyes as we walked over to our car, I am sure he followed us to the safe house just to make sure his niece was okay. As we drove to the safe house Oliana kept looking around nervously to see if we were being followed.

Oliana began to relax when we arrived at the safe house. Sam and Darleen who operated the safe house greeted us with warmth and kindness. They clarified the purpose of the house and explained the house rules. Oliana was very grateful to have a safe place to stay; therefore she was more than willing to accept the rules. After we chatted for a while, Oliana turned to Clifford and I and said, "I am sorry for the way I behaved when you approached me on the street. I knew in my heart that you were concerned for me and the other women but I did not want to admit I was doing anything wrong. When you gave me the testimony booklet I was going to throw it away but something inside of me said "hold on to this booklet you many need it one day".

The Enforcer

Oliana's pimp's enforcer was an unscrupulous ruthless man who had recently brutally beat up one of her friends. When the women did not bring enough money home he would beat them up and send them back out on the street to meet their quota. Generally the quota for each woman was $1,500.00 a night. It is well known in the high track area that the pimps controlled the prostitutes through fear and manipulation. Oliana was not on good terms with her pimp because she wanted to get out of her contract. Oliana paid him an extra percent of her earnings every month so she could leave prostitution. She knew that it was only a matter of time before he would silence her with a beating.

One evening while the enforcer was involved elsewhere, she mustered up enough courage to slip away and hide out at a friend's apartment. While she was at her friend's apartment she found out that her pimp had put a contract out on her. She knew that she would eventually be beaten or even killed.

During my counselling visits to the safe home Oliana shared her story. When she was a young teenager her parents divorced. Oliana's mother moved to Victoria and left her with her father; unfortunately Oliana never felt loved by either parent. When she was fifteen she ran away to Victoria, to be with her mother. Her mother was too busy finding her own niche in life; sadly she didn't have time for her daughter. Consequently their relationship began to deteriorate. Oliana was so hungry for love and acceptance that she reached out to her peers, especially young men for emotional security and love.

The Bait

At the age of seventeen Oliana ran away from her mother's home right into the arms of a flashy guy who told her what she wanted to hear. In order to justify her actions she told herself that her mother would be happier without her as a burden. Slowly she was drawn under this man's control with empty promises of money, clothes, diamonds and furs. Unfortunately she fell for the bait. Oliana did not know that this unscrupulous man dealt in human trafficking. After grooming her for several months he sold her to a pimp. Oliana was led to believe that she was this pimp's number one girl, but later on she found out that he had many number one women working for him around Georgia Street near the Vancouver Hotel. This really burst her bubble of feeling important and loved. Oliana was so upset that she ran off to Calgary where she ended up working for other pimps.

For several years she bounced back and forth from pimp to pimp, city to city. When she moved back into Vancouver she came under the control of a group called The Family. This particular pimp was very forceful; he demanded that the women sign a contract giving him a percentage of all they earned. He hired an enforcer to control his investments. The enforcer checked up on the women and collected the money.

Oliana's health was deteriorating due to using drugs, alcohol, and working late nights on the streets in all kinds of weather. The fear of being beaten up or killed griped her and she knew she had to escape. She prayed and asked God to help her. As she was praying she reached down into her pocket and found Crossfire's booklet. Hope sprung up within her as she recalled the conversations she had with our team. She knew that God heard her prayers and would help her escape.

A Big Adjustment

Living in a Christian family environment was a big adjustment for Oliana because there was no swearing, drinking, or partying. For the first three months the only place Oliana went was to Church. She had to stay close to home in order to avoid being found by her ex-pimp. After she had been at the safe house for six months she went shopping at Metrotown Mall with Darlene. While they were shopping Oliana saw her ex-pimp; he was buying clothes for a young woman. Oliana thought she was going to faint from fear; she quickly hid behind Darlene and quietly told her that her ex-pimp was about a hundred feet away from them. Fortunately they managed to leave without being seen. This experience was so traumatic that Oliana was afraid to leave the house for several days.

After ten months, Oliana assumed that her ex-pimp would have given up looking for her; therefore she felt free go on outings. There were several occasions when she came home drunk and disorderly and disrupted the whole household. This type of behavior did not go down well with Sam and Darlene. Oliana would apologize for her behavior but yet again she would go out with her friends and arrive home in a drunken state. Finally, Oliana realized she needed to respect this home and the wonderful godly people who cared for her.

While Oliana lived at the safe house I was responsible to counsel and support her in her recovery. Several times I had to mediate between Oliana and Darlene. I am sure that these dear people had no idea of the time and patience it would take to care for an ex-prostitute. But Sam and Darlene were committed to assist Oliana through her recovery and schooling. During her time at the safe house Oliana attended church and gave her life to the Lord.

Sabotage

Oliana signed up for a six month meat cutting and wrapping course with BCIT. This course included on the job training at various major grocery stores. Oliana became despondent and discouraged with her progress, and she was afraid that she might not pass her exams. Two nights before her final exam, Oliana went out with her friends and got drunk. Oliana was so afraid of failing her exam that she sabotaged her success; regrettably she did fail her exam.

There was no more money for education so Oliana had to find a job. The reality of working an entry level job hit Oliana hard. She had never worked a regular job so the big question was what was she going to put on her resume? How was she going to explain why she had not worked or had any experience for any type of work?

The reality of applying for work was so depressing that all she wanted to do was hide away in bed. In her depressed state she said to me, "Bernice I need to find out if I belong down on the streets or in regular society." I knew that this was a very dangerous decision but we had to let her figure it out. While she was visiting her old stomping grounds she was sickened by the thought of returning to prostitution. She returned to the safe house with a more sober attitude; she was willing to cooperate with the house parents and the rules of the house. In order to earn money for her education she worked as a part time nanny and part time waitress.

Roller Coaster Ride

Oliana went home for Christmas. Her visit with her family did not go well; there seemed to be a lot of bickering and drinking. Oliana could see the contrast between a loving Christian family and her very dysfunctional family. When Oliana came back to the safe house Darlene noticed that Oliana was very discontented. Nothing seemed to satisfy her. She was worried about her finances, she started drinking and hanging out with a rough crowd, and eventually she lost her jobs.

I knew that Oliana was in trouble when she arrived at church drunk. She was very emotional and cried a lot during the service. I took her out for lunch and tried to discover what her problem was, but she didn't want to talk about it. She told me that she was going downtown to see her old friends, I tried to stop her but she wouldn't listen to me. Once again I felt very helpless; all I could do was to commit her to the Lord. That same evening she came back to the safe house with a humble attitude. She said to Darlene and Sam, "I now know that you have my best interest at heart, please forgive me for my miserable behavior".

In January Oliana discovered that she was pregnant. Oliana confessed to the house parents that while she was visiting her family at Christmas she had an affair with her ex- boyfriend. Oliana knew she had made a big mistake, but she was determined to keep the baby. Oliana was not interested in marrying this man; therefore she did not want him to know that she was pregnant.

The Challenge

Oliana became conscious of the fact that supporting a child was going to be a challenge. She knew that she had to upgrade her education seriously. Oliana made an appointment with a career counselor at BCIT and arranged to take a computer course. The policy at the safe house was that women were able to stay in the home during their pregnancy, but they would have to leave three months after the birth of their baby. The house parents told Oliana it was up to her whether she left or stayed during her pregnancy. The decision was not easy for Oliana because did not like living by rules of the house and she was still in danger from her pimp. Fortunately, Oliana decided to stay at the safe house but there were many arguments regarding food, housekeeping and attending bible study. Finally she settled down and accepted the rules and routine of the house. Oliana worked two part-time jobs as well as attending school.

In August 1992 the house parents invited the Crossfire Ministry team to celebrate Oliana's one year freedom from prostitution. I am sure the Lord has a crown of gold for this wonderful couple. They are a great example of patience and love toward all the women they have cared for over the years.

Single Mother

In September 1992 Oliana gave birth to a beautiful baby girl. The house parents and I felt like proud grandparents to this child. Crossfire Ministries had just opened their own recovery home and invited Oliana to live in this home. Oliana declined because she did not want to bring up her child in a home for ex-prostitutes and drug addicts. The reality of leaving the security of Darlene and Sam's safe house and facing the unknown life as a single mother was overwhelming. Her only option was to venture out on her own and find a small apartment. Fortunately she found a place near me and close to the safe house. This made it more convenient to assist her when she needed help.

In order to attend school Oliana needed a baby sitter. We both prayed and asked the Lord for a baby sitter who could work with Oliana's school schedule. The Lord not only answered our prayers, but directed Oliana to a very nice lady who lived in her apartment building. This dear woman loved children and agreed to work for a reasonable wage.

The first year as a single mother was very hard. Oliana didn't realize that babies needed so much attention. Oliana's new life consisted of school, part-time work and a new baby. She found herself constantly tired, depressed, and lonely. But she was determined to get her education even if it meant that she had no social life. She would often phone me crying, "I have no life, is this all there is to life?" Lack of finances was always a problem, but she would rather work in a restaurant and earn low wages than return to prostitution. Crossfire Ministries supported Oliana over the years by paying her rent when her finances were low and purchasing groceries when the cupboard was bare. After three years of schooling Oliana graduated in Office Administration. She obtained a good job with the government and finally earned enough money to support herself and her daughter.

A New Church

The large church Oliana attended was impressive, but she felt that it was too big to build close relationships with the people. She desired a more intimate fellowship with people her age; therefore she moved to a small Baptist church. Oliana asked me if I would attend this church with her because she was nervous about attending on her own. I agreed to attend church with her until she developed some close relationships within the church. The church people were very friendly and embraced Oliana and her baby. It was a great blessing for me to witness Oliana's spiritual growth.

The Lord answered many prayers for Oliana during those difficult years. But there was one prayer that appeared to be unanswered; it was her prayer for a Christian husband. It was difficult for Oliana to wait for a Christian husband. Remember, Oliana is a very beautiful woman and many men wanted to take her out, but she knew that only a Christian man would do. Oliana's obedience in only wanting a Christian husband paid off; God answered her prayers. After attending the Baptist church for two years, the Lord brought a great single man into the church; they started to build a relationship, fell in love, and got married.

Today Oliana has two children, a wonderful husband, a lovely home and she is doing well at her job. Oliana's relationship with her parents has dramatically changed; it took forgiveness, healing and acceptance on everyone's part. It took years of perseverance, change of attitude, and God's love and mercy for Oliana to step from the world of prostitution into God's destiny for her life.

As I step back and contemplate the handiwork of God in Oliana's life I am amazed at how Jesus so gently changed her life. *"And then take on an entirely new way of life – a God fashioned life, a life renewed from the inside and working itself into your conduct as God accurately reproduces His character in you"*. *(Ephesians 4, 24)*

Diane

"That Woman Was Me."

I was attending Crossfire Ministry's booth at Missionfest in Vancouver when a young women with a little girl in a stroller stopped at the booth. She was strikingly beautiful with bright red hair, delicate features, large blue eyes, and a slim figure. She appeared as if she were in a trance. She stood still with her eyes fixated on a large picture that was the backdrop of our booth. The picture was a charcoal drawing of the Bible story about a woman caught in adultery. As I watched Diane I saw a look of sadness come over her face; she looked as if she was about to cry. When her little girl started to fuss Diane took her eyes off the picture and attended to her daughter. I approached Diane and introduced myself, then I handed her one of the ministries brochures. She looked it over and then looked back at the picture. Then she turned to me and said, "that woman was me." Diane sat down on a chair beside our booth and told me some of her story.

I realized that this was not the place for her to share intimate details of her life so I gave her my phone number and set up an appointment.

The following week I met Diane at a small restaurant; she was eager to talk to someone who understood and cared for her. She had carried her burden in silence for a long time and now she could freely tell her story.

Diane did not go into much detail about her family except that it was dysfunctional and unstable. In her early teens she moved out of her home and found a cheap apartment. She supported herself by working two jobs as well as attending school. When she was nineteen years old, a well-dressed older man approached her at her work place and offered her $500.00 to spend the evening with him. He offered her $200.00 for her to think about it and $300.00 more if she showed up at his hotel room. Diane thought to herself, "this would be more money than I could earn in a month. The temptation was just too great so I brushed aside my inner feelings of fear. Once I walked through that hotel door I knew there was no turning back."

Diane made the rounds of the big hotels and conventions centers where there were many traveling businessmen looking for a good time. She worked on her own for a while until the security officers got wise to what she was doing. Diane decided to connect with an escort agency which provided her with customers but took a slice of the money she earned. Most of her customers were wealthy men who took her out to expensive places. Diane got caught up in the dazzling excitement of parties, rich men, and drugs. She thought, "wow this is the high life working for $200 an hour." But deep down, she knew that this destructive life style and its money had control over her.

Diane's life became a blur. She began to feel sick about working in prostitution, but she was so consumed by the money that she could not quit. Diane was now in a predicament; she began loathing the calls from the escort agency so she worked less, and spent more time at parties using alcohol and drugs. At one of the parties she met a man who she thought was the answer to leaving prostitution. They went to Europe together but the relationship quickly deteriorated. Diane returned to Canada and resumed working for an escort agency.

Hooked

Diane told me that drug addiction is really sneaky. It hangs around the edge of your life, then, seemingly without warning it grabs you and before you realize it you are hooked. Diane's drug habit dominated her life to the point that she was not able to work therefore the escort agency cancelled their contract with her. This was a blow to Diane because she now had to find another way to make money. Diane contacted a friend who was involved in street prostitution; her friend showed her the ropes of street prostitution. Soliciting on the street was inhospitable, standing out on the street in all kinds of weather; competing with the other women, and working for less money. There was also the problem of pimps trying to recruit her. Diane told me that it was like going to hell in a hand basket. After a short period of time she decided that street prostitution had too many problems; she had to find a different method to attract customers so she placed an advertisement in a newspaper and used her cell phone as a contact for customers.

The Thought of Dying

Diane became aware that over the years the quality of the drugs had deteriorated; it was often laced with foreign substances that could kill her. She was afraid that she would end up dead in some back alley. She told me, "I knew somewhere deep inside me that if I was to die and meet God, I would be in a big mess." The thought of dying continued to haunt her, she knew that she needed to deal with her addiction.

She made an attempt by attending Narcotics Anonymous meetings. For a year she went through a period of staying clean, then relapsing and working in prostitution. Finally, she realized that she had to make a clean break from prostitution and drugs. Breaking free was a struggle, no money and no drugs, but she faithfully attended the NA meetings. The NA and AA program teach addicts to turn their lives over to the God of their understanding. This was very foreign to Diane, she questioned why turning her life over to God would change anything. Diane thought to herself, "I am going to test God and ask Him to change my life." During our interview a few years later she told me "God did not chase me down and assault me because I was doing wrong; He simply stayed available, and continued to invite me into a relationship with Himself. This was a relationship of unconditional love. God offered me forgiveness for the wrong and harmful life choices I made. God offered me acceptance and promised me a life of meaning and purpose that didn't depend on money. God did not barge in and yank away control of my life; but when I submitted my life to God's care He really did change my life."

The Love of Jesus

While Diane attended church in her neighborhood she received Jesus as her Saviour. Diane's encounter with Jesus was genuine; she gave up drugs and prostitution without any hesitation. The love of Jesus flooded into her life like healing ointment. *"Bless the Lord, O my soul who forgives all your iniquities and heals all your diseases; who redeems your life from destruction." (Psalm 103:1, 3, 4)*

Diane and I met together for Bible study and counselling. I was amazed at her hunger to learn about Jesus and understand the Bible.

Down But Not Defeated

Diane absolutely adored her daughter who was an inquisitive bright child. Diane couldn't stand the thought of working away from home and leaving her daughter with a baby-sitter. So she decided to have a small day-care in her home. Much to her surprise she enjoyed looking after children. She felt that child care would be a good career choice so she took a Child Care course at Trinity

Western University. Being without a car and finances was a problem so she gave up the course. Diane was down but not defeated; she committed her situation to the Lord. The Bible verse she held onto was *"Be anxious for nothing, but in everything by prayer and supplication, with thanksgiving, let your requests be made known to God; and the peace of God, which surpasses all understanding, will guard your hearts and minds through Christ Jesus." (Phil 4:6)*

God heard Diane's prayer and opened another door for her to take a correspondence course for a Day Care manager. After she graduated she turned her basement into a Day Care. It seemed as if everything was going well. Diane was happy with the Day Care Center but she was lonely and desired to have a husband.

Broken Heart

Diane met a man at church whom she thought was the man of her dreams but unfortunately he was not interested in marriage; he only wanted Diane to live with him. Once again she felt let down, and outcast because of her background. Diane very firmly let this man know that she would not enter into a common law relationship. With a broken heart, she reached out to the Lord for comfort. Diane decided that she could no longer fellowship in this church so she left the church. Fortunately, she found another church that embraced her and her daughter.

The changes in Diane's life are commendable; she is a woman of strong faith and a great mother. Diane is an inspiration to many young single women in her church. God has put order back into Diane's life because she gave Him control; He is Lord of her life. I have lost touch with Diane but I am sure one day that we will meet again and rejoice over God's love and mercy in her life. I believe that this portion of scripture is for Diane.

"I waited patiently for the Lord; And He inclined to me, And heard my cry. He also brought me up out of a horrible pit, Out of the miry clay,

And set my feet upon a rock, And established my steps. He has put a new song in my mouth—Praise to our God; Many will see it and fear, And will trust in the LORD. (Psalm 40:1 & 2)

Chapter 9

Gerry – A Desperate Call

On a cool September evening, while I was walking up Keefer Street with a ministry partner, I heard someone calling, "wait, wait, wait, I want to talk to you". I turned around to see a young woman running towards us. By the time she reached us she couldn't talk; she doubled over to catch her breath. The anguish in her face touched my heart. I waited until she caught her breath and then I asked, "How can we help you?" Immediately she said, "please get me out of here I can't take it anymore". Gerry was about twenty three years old. She was petite, with short light blond hair, a slim figure, and she was dressed in a light blue jacket and jeans.

Gerry told us that she had been using cocaine and had been in prostitution for eight years. She said that she was at a point where she could no longer continue; it was either treatment or suicide. Fortunately, one of our safe house workers joined our team that night, therefore we were able to assess Gerry's situation. The policy of admission to the safe house was that all clients had to be detoxed for at least one month before they could be admitted. The safe house worker felt that Gerry's situation was an emergency; therefore it was decided to admit Gerry into the Safe house on a trial basis.

Swore Like a Sailor

Unbeknownst to us, Gerry would be a great challenge to our house workers. Within the first week they learned a whole new vocabulary of swear words. Gerry swore like a sailor. She openly admitted that she was gay, that she did not believe in God, and that she had no intentions of changing her beliefs. During the devotional time she would sit at the back of the group with her arms crossed looking very defiant. Despite her attitude, we all loved Gerry. I respected her raw honesty regarding how she felt about things; Gerry did not play the performance pleasing game.

The first month in the safe house was brutal for the staff because Gerry was suspicious of everyone. She did not engage with the other women and she tried to get out of all the programs, especially the Christian activities.

Finally, she warmed up to the house workers and the other women. Gerry lived in the safe house for approximately one year, and within that time she completed the first four steps of the twelve step program and most of the other programs. When Gerry did not want to cooperate she would have a major temper tantrum using many colorful words. The house director's patience was admirable; she was caring and loving in many ways. Many times throughout Gerry's stay the staff paid for Gerry's haircuts and clothes out of their own salary.

After several weeks in the safe house Gerry let down her guard and shared her story. Gerry was adopted into a Christian family whose main ministry was to help people caught in cults to refocus their lives. Tragically, there was very little positive Christian teaching and love in the home. Gerry became very confused regarding her religious direction; it all seemed hypocritical. All she wanted was to be loved and to feel secure.

When Gerry became a

teenager she sought for love in all the wrong places. When her parents found out that she was gay and using drugs they asked her to leave their home. Gerry became a street kid begging for food and sleeping on the street. She could not earn enough money begging to feed her drug habit so she entered into prostitution. After several years in prostitution she became hardened to any form of love or friendship. Her objective was to use people for her benefit, but this behaviour did not win her any friends.

Gerry worked through the programs but she still did not seem to have a change of heart. She still resisted God's love and mercy towards her. In spite of Gerry's attitude toward God she responded to the love of the house workers and she valued the work that was being done for all the women in the house.

When Gerry had completed a year in the program she felt that it was time to leave. She was now ready to face her new life without drugs. On one hand it was a relief to see her move on, but she left a big hole in our hearts.

About a year later, while I was ministering in the East Hasting area I saw Gerry walking toward me. At first I thought, "oh God I hope she has not returned to prostitution and drugs". As she approached me she had a big smile on her face. We hugged and both said at the same time, "what are you doing here?" Gerry explained to me that she was involved with a group in the area that was assisting women in getting out of prostitution and off drugs. She said, "now I know how hard it is to help people turn their lives around; the shoe is on the other foot. Now I am the one trying to convince women that there is hope and love in this world. It is my turn to share my story of recovery and hope."

I asked Gerry if her opinion of God had changed. Her answer was, "Yes, I now believe in God but I still have my doubts about why Jesus would love someone like me." Then I shared how Jesus love for her was unconditional.

Gerry didn't want to let me go, but she had to leave because she did not want to be late for work at the East-side Recovery Center. Gerry asked me if I would like to meet the staff, so I went into the building with her. The office was small with a receiving desk, a couple of tables, some chairs, and a couch. There were several women resting on the couch. Gerry introduced me to the staff and the women; she told them that I was the person who helped her get off drugs and prostitution. I shared a few interesting stories about Gerry's recovery at the safe house.

When it was time for me to leave, Gerry walked out of the building with me. At the door I turned to her and asked if I could pray for her. She immediately said "yes." As I was praying, I noticed that her old obstinate spirit had gone; Gerry's head was bowed and there were tears in her eyes. I hugged her and went on my way with the feeling that Gerry was on the right path, the path and destiny that Jesus had planned for her.

I have not seen Gerry since that time but I will never forget this feisty woman who ran after us to get off the streets. Even though her behaviour at the safe house was tumultuous, God put a love in our hearts that overlooked her outward behaviour.

My prayer for Gerry is that she will continue to seek and know Jesus who loves her with an everlasting love. *"Ask, and it will be given to you; seek, and you will find; knock and it will be opened to you. For everyone who asks receives, and he who seeks finds, and to him who knocks it will be opened. (Matthew 7: 7 - 8)*

Vanessa "That's Me"

In September 1998 I was asked to interview a teenage woman who was interested in entering Crossfire's recovery house. I arranged to meet Vanessa on Friday at eleven a.m. at a local restaurant. After waiting for thirty minutes, I thought to myself, "she is a no show; I may as well go home." I paid my bill for the coffee and put my on jacket. When I was about to leave, a young woman about eighteen years old walked up to me and said, "are you Bernice?" I replied, "Yes, and are you Vanessa?" With a smile on her face, she said, "That's me." I noticed that she was twitchy; I thought to myself, "Oh no! She is high on cocaine". Vanessa was of medium height; she had a sweet round face, brown eyes, and brown curly hair. She was dressed in modern black baggy pants, white hoody, and new white sneakers.

We sat down at a booth and ordered a beverage. I asked her why she wanted to enter the recovery house; she told me that she was tired of the cycle of drugs and prostitution. I explained to Vanessa the rules and restrictions of living in a recovery house. She agreed to cooperate, so I made an appointment for her to meet the house director. After two weeks in detox Vanessa was ready to move into the safe house.

Free Spirit

Rules and restrictions had not been part of Vanessa's life. Even though she signed a contract to obey the policies of the house, she still found it difficult to adhere to them. After several weeks, she settled down and began adjusting to the house policies and daily programs. I was Vanessa's counselor and sounding board. I enjoyed our sessions together; she was always upbeat and full of fun. She did not hold back when she shared her story during our counseling sessions.

Vanessa's story was very similar to many of the stories I heard over the years. She grew up in a dysfunctional home. Her mother was in and out of relationships. She did not have time for her children, therefore the children brought themselves up. There were no rules in her home; she could come and go as she pleased. Vanessa told me that she was sexually abused by one of her mother's boyfriends. This devastating experience set the stage for her young life. In

101

her early teens Vanessa vowed to herself that if anyone wanted to sexually use her, they would have to pay for it.

Birds of a Feather Flock Together

Vanessa friends were all living free from parental guidance. Vanessa's best friend was Lilly, a drug dealer and prostitute. It wasn't long before Vanessa was using cocaine, and dealing drugs. Vanessa's addiction was getting out of control; she ran out of things to steal and sell. The drug dealers no longer trusted her because she used too much of their product.

When her mother realized that her daughter was an out of control drug addict she kicked her out of the house. Vanessa felt that her only option was to move in with Lilly. Lilly set Vanessa up with her first date. He was an older man who paid her eighty dollars for the trick. He took her out to a nice restaurant and after, he took her to a place where she could score some cocaine. Lilly eased Vanessa into the sex trade by making the first experience a pleasant one. Lilly told Vanessa, "See, it wasn't too bad; they take you to a nice restaurant and you give them sex, then they pay you and take you wherever you want."

Most of her dates were indoors and by appointment, -- "sugar daddies that paid good money". At the end of the night she would party, use drugs, and laugh it up with friends. She told me her life was spiraling out of control. The more drugs she used, the more money she needed. Even her appearance changed because she was so doped up. The johns didn't want to pay big money anymore because she was high on drugs. She had to work longer hours in order to make enough money.

Twisted Thinking

Vanessa had several bad dates; she was beaten, robbed, and left in places out of town. I asked Vanessa why she continued on this path when it was evident that the world she was living in was so dark and destructive. She said to me, "It wasn't just for money and drugs, I did it for validation. Some may think I had an addiction to sex but it was for my customer's admiration of my skills as a prostitute". Here was a young woman so misled and confused that she used sex to validate her identity.

Did Jesus Really Die for Me?

Vanessa often went to church with me; she seemed interested in the worship and in the message. One Sunday during the communion service she asked me if she should take communion. I explained to her what communion meant, she bowed her head and said, "did Jesus really die for the sins of the whole world; does that include my sin?" I told her, "yes." That very morning Vanessa asked Jesus to forgive her for her sin and to come into her life. When the service was over I introduced Vanessa to the pastor and she prayed for her.

After this experience Vanessa's attitude changed for the good; she was happy and cooperative at the safe house. Vanessa had a wonderful sense of humor; we had many great laughs together. She was full of fun; we called her monkey because she loved to scale the hallway walls with her feet and hands on each side of the walls.

Vanessa lived in the house for about eight months, completing most of the programs. She was anxious to get on with her life and go back to high school, so she made arrangements to live with another woman who had completed the program and was ready to move on. Things seemed to go well for a while, but the two women did not get along, so Vanessa moved out and moved back to Lilly's place. The move to Lilly's place was disastrous. Once again, Vanessa found herself on the old treadmill of drugs and prostitution. This is a quote from Vanessa, "prostitution is easy to get into, but tough to get out of. Prostitution is an addiction just like drugs and booze.

Once you get into the whirlpool you spiral out of control; there is nowhere to go but down."

Vanessa made several attempts to straighten herself out by entering treatment centers, but she always left because of money. Money was her security blanket. Vanessa called me several times to let me know that she was alive.

Throughout the years, we often met for coffee and a chat. During one of our visits, I noticed that Vanessa was acting very strange; she had become paranoid; she thought people were spying on her everywhere she went. I knew the drugs were affecting her brain. I told her that she needed to see her doctor and be referred to a Psychiatrist. She called me many times with stories of seeing strange things in her room. I would pray with her and she would calm down. Eventually, Vanessa realized that she was going off the deep end mentally. She went to the doctor and was placed on medication. I am happy to say that she is now doing fine and is back on the road to a normal life. Vanessa speaks at local high schools, sharing her story with the hope of preventing other teens from entering the trap of drugs and prostitution.

Vanessa and I stay in touch by phone and e-mail. I am always thrilled to see and hear about the great changes in her life. Vanessa has been clean and sober for several years. She now works as a volunteer at several youth centers.

Vanessa never gave up on her faith even when she was at the bottom of the pit. She knew that God would bring her through her dark and sick days. God never gave up on his daughter; His love and mercy for Vanessa is profound.

"What I have said, that will I bring about; what I have planned that will I do." (Isaiah 46:11b) I believe that God has special plans for Vanessa's life.

Dawn

Dawn was one tough, independent woman. She was unapproachable and didn't trust anyone. She would beat up other prostitutes and even her customers. Most of the street missionaries were afraid to approach her because she would tell them in many obscene words to leave her alone.

During my sixteen years as a Street Missionary, I met many interesting women. Dawn seemed to be the most challenging of them all. Due to her violent reputation, Dawn did not have many women friends. Sally was the exception. Her gentle nature was opposite to Dawn's uncompromising attitude. Both women were strikingly beautiful. Dawn was African American, thirty four years old, oval face, brown eyes, long black hair, medium height with a slim figure. She was always dressed in beautiful clothes and spike heels. When she smiled, her whole face would light up.

Sally was twenty eight, long blond hair, beautiful blue eyes, tall, with a soft voice and welcoming smile, but there was sadness in her eyes that was haunting. Sally was always willing to talk to our team while Dawn stood back and listened.

Tragedy Strikes

Sally was devastated by the death of her baby girl who had been in foster care. Dawn called Crossfire regarding the situation. She told us that Sally was overwhelmed with the funeral arrangements and she was not coping very well emotionally. Crossfire's team assisted with the funeral arrangements and with spiritual support. One of the team members built a beautiful coffin for the deceased baby. On the day of the funeral, the weather was overcast and raining. During the funeral service, Sally shook with deep sobs. It was so painful to see her in such anguish; my heart was breaking for her.

After the funeral, Sally stayed with Dawn. Dawn couldn't afford to keep her very long because she had to care for her own children, a girl, eight years old and a boy, four years old. Once again, the Crossfire team stepped in and provided food and money. When Dawn saw the love of God in action, her attitude toward us changed. Dawn and the children looked forward to our visits. When she encountered us on the street she was always happy to talk. Sally left Vancouver and moved back to her parent's home.

Intense Anger

As I began to know Dawn, I realized that there was deep anger within her. I asked myself, "why is this woman so angry, and what has driven her into a life of crime, drugs, and prostitution?" Perhaps this poem written by Dawn is the answer.

Heart & Soul in Motion

My life is a torment in itself

Torment and pain

Agony and shame

Seem to follow me with each passing day.

Dawn's background started with her birth, in London, England's east-side. Her father was a business man who traveled all over the world. He was very abusive to his wife, who transferred her anger to Dawn and her brother. Dawn said, "I don't know why my mother disliked me so much." At the age of five, Dawn's mother beat Dawn over the head with a cooking spoon because she was eating too slowly. Dawn was taken to the hospital with a severe gash on the top of her head.

At a very young age, Dawn was sexually abused by her older brother. She tried to bury her shame but finally, she told her mother. Her brother denied it and her mother believed him. The family moved back and forth from England to Nigeria. At the age of twelve Dawn's family moved to London Ontario. When Dawn was thirteen years old, the family moved to Edmonton. Dawn seemed to have a lot of unrelated uncles living in her home. Every time a new man moved in she was to call him uncle. Life at home had become unbearable because Dawn and her siblings were constantly being beaten for every little thing.

A Short Lived Reprieve

When Dawn's uncle and aunt came to visit the family Dawn begged her uncle and aunt to take her home with them. Dawn was fifteen when she moved to Winnipeg with her uncle and aunt; they all lived in a small two bedroom apartment. For the first time in her life, she felt free from her overbearing mother and all the violence in the home.

Instead of enjoying her freedom in a sensible way she abused her freedom by running wild. She hung around with other young people who didn't attend school. Dawn became involved with an older man and she eventually became pregnant. After breaking the news to her uncle, it was decided that she should have an abortion. The aunt and uncle were very disappointed with Dawn and soon after her abortion they sent her home to her mother.

Downward Misfortunes

Dawn's mother gave her a very cold reception and once again treated her badly. During a fight with her mother, Dawn was stabbed in her left arm. Dawn realized that it was no longer safe to live at home, so she ran away. Dawn did not have any place to live, so she would walk, ride buses and trains looking for a place to stay for the night. In order for find shelter, she ended up staying with people who abused her sexually. An older man, Jack, befriended Dawn and invited her to a party; she had no idea that the purpose of this party was to use her for prostitution.

Dawn met another man, who she thought loved her, but after she became pregnant he took off. She was eighteen when she gave birth to a baby boy. At first she was happy with her baby but after a while she realized that she was not able to care for him. Because her life was so filled with crime, drugs, incarceration and prostitution, she knew that this was no life for a child so she asked her mother to take care of the baby. Initially her mother agreed, but ended up giving the baby away.

Dawn was in and out of several relationships and when she was twenty three she became pregnant again. This time she had a baby girl. Dawn decided to keep her baby and asked her mother to give her, son back. Her mother told her that she gave him up for adoption; she would not tell Dawn where her son was. No one in the family would help her find her son. Several years later she gave birth to another baby boy.

Dawn moved from Winnipeg to Edmonton, and then to Calgary. Each place and each relationship seemed to have its problems. There was no stability in Dawn's life because of drugs, prostitution, and abusive men.

In 1992, Dawn moved to Vancouver, arriving at the bus terminal with two small children and no place to live. She called a women's shelter and stayed there for one month. Then she stayed in a motel for two weeks until she found an apartment. Welfare was not enough to pay for rent, food, and drugs, so she contacted an old acquaintance and went back into prostitution.

God's Providence

I had no idea that Dawn and I were destined to become great friends. In the beginning, our relationship was sporadic, because

109

every few months she would move to a new location. When she required help she would call Crossfire's office. In response, we assisted her with food for her children. Crossfire always made sure that her family received a Christmas hamper with food and toys for the children.

One beautiful spring day, I drove Dawn and her two children to Stanley Park. The children were very excited because this was their first visit to Stanley Park. As we were driving through the park the children were glued to the car window, calling out "look, mom, look!" As soon as we stopped the car at Second Beach, the children scrambled out of the car and ran toward the beach. The children thoroughly enjoyed themselves, climbing over rocks and playing in the sand. Dawn seemed to be a totally different woman as she laughed and played with the children. I was so amazed that this tough woman from the streets could raise such well-behaved children. After we ate our picnic lunch, we sat back and enjoyed the beautiful day.

Throughout our visit to Stanley Park, God impressed on me that He wanted me to embrace this family. I often visited Dawn in her home and shared the gospel with her, but she had her own ideas about spiritual things. It was all mixed up with voodoo, superstition, and God.

When Dawn moved from Vancouver to Surrey, I found visiting her a bit challenging so we kept in touch by phone. Several times she could not talk to me on the phone because she was drunk, drug sick, or depressed. It was evident that her addiction was spiraling out of control. Instead of Dawn looking after her children, they were now looking after her.

Closing the Door

Finally Dawn had enough; she was in poor health and sick of her life style. We talked about her closing the door to prostitution and ending an unhealthy relationship. I knew that Dawn was at a crossroad and would need a lot of support and encouragement. Once Dawn left prostitution her health and her relationship with her children improved.

My friendship with Dawn was challenging at times because little things would trigger an explosive reaction. There were times when I felt uncomfortable being with her because she would lash out at people in stores or restaurants for treating her in a discriminatory way. On several occasions she got right in the person's face and let them know what she thought about their actions. Dawn was a fighter and was not going to let people put her down. To my amazement she never lashed out at me when I corrected her regarding her behavior or attitude.

Reconciliation

The relationship between Dawn and her older brother had been strained for years because of sexual abuse. Her brother wanted to make restitution for his actions toward Dawn; therefore he admitted that what he did was immoral. Her bother passed away before she had an opportunity to forgive him. While Dawn was attending her brother's funeral she met her eldest son who was now nineteen years old. The family had secretly placed her son into the care of an uncle who lived in Ontario. A month after the funeral Dawn's son came to Vancouver to live with her.

Dawn was delighted to finally have her son with her, but it wasn't long before their relationship started to deteriorate. Regrettably, her son did not see the need to work; he felt that he was above manual labour. His influence over his teenage sister was detrimental because she absolutely adored him and got caught up in his egotistical attitude. When Dawn found out that he was selling drugs, she had to make a difficult decision. Dawn had been clean from drug addiction for several years and would not allow drugs in the house.

This was a heart breaking decision but in order to protect her other children she had to tell him to leave her home. He moved into a hotel near Powell Street and set up a drug distribution center.

After her son left home, tensions grew between Dawn and her teenage daughter. Her daughter, was extremely angry with Dawn for removing her brother from their home. She became defiant, disrespectful, demanding money, and skipping out of school. The fact that Dawn was drinking a lot didn't help their relationship. Dawn realized she needed help with her daughter, so they went for mediation and counselling. Dawn promised her daughter that she would stop drinking, but even this did not heal their relationship. Their relationship deteriorated to the point that Dawn had her daughter removed from the home. Dawn's daughter would return on and off but they never seemed to have any kind of cordial relationship.

New Career Dashed

Dawn took a course as a nail technician; after she graduated she got some part time work. Her job gave her confidence and her future looked good until tragedy hit. Dawn broke her hand and was not able to continue with her job. She had surgery but the Surgeon botched the operation. Unfortunately she lost normal function of her hand. With all her education money gone, she had to find a level entry job that didn't require a steady hand. Due to her criminal record, she had to work for companies who did not require a criminal check. This often led to working for people who paid low wages.

Encounter with Jesus

When the movie *The Passion of the Christ*, was playing in the theater, I invited Dawn to the movie. I was surprised when she agreed to go. Before we went to the movie, I prayed that the Lord would use this film to speak to Dawn's heart. While we were watching the movie, I would sneak a peek at Dawn to see her reaction. She was watching so intensely that she barely moved, but every now and then, Dawn would wipe her eyes. Along with many other people in the theater, we were both crying softly.

When the movie was over and we were walking back into the mall, I asked Dawn if she wanted to stop for a coffee. She mumbled, "No, I want to go home." I noticed that she was in a daze and was walking as if she were drunk but I knew that she had not been drinking. It was apparent that she was under the power of the Holy Spirit. When we got on the Sky Train, she was very quiet. I asked her what she thought of the movie. She quietly said, "I now understand forgiveness. I know that for me to have a relationship with Jesus, I have to forgive my family for all the abuse and abandonment they inflicted on me." It wasn't long after the movie that Dawn turned her heart and life over to Jesus Christ.

Heartbreak

Shortly after Dawn's son moved to Vancouver he was murdered in a drug related incident. This was a crushing blow for Dawn; she could not wrap her mind around the fact that her twenty one year old son was dead. Dawn's grief was amplified by her family because they blamed her for his death.

My pastor and church friends officiated at the funeral service. The funeral chapel was filled with young people who knew Dawn's son but the only family member who attended was Dawn's sister. It was a difficult funeral; sorrow filled the room with people weeping. My heart was heavy for Dawn and her children; I found it difficult to hold back my tears.

Friends from my church prepared a luncheon at Dawn's home. The atmosphere in the house was gloomy, and somber; it felt like all the life had been sucked out of the house. Dawn's sister tried to comfort

Dawn's daughter, but she would have nothing to do with her aunt. Dawn's daughter fled to her bedroom weeping, uncontrollably. I followed her into her bedroom and held her as she wept. Dawn tried to contain her grief by serving the luncheon and talking to people, but the overwrought look on her face was unmistakable.

The Murder Trial

The police investigation intensified after the funeral. When Dawn saw the pictures of her son's body, beaten and riddled with bullets, her emotional distress became so intense that she had to be put on medication. Dawn's many interviews; with the prosecuting attorney for the murder trial was very stressful. Finally the trial was set; I accompanied Dawn to the court house and held her hand as the evidence was brought forth. We were both relieved when the jury found the accused guilty of manslaughter and sentenced him to fifteen years in prison, but the accused's lawyer appealed the case. The second trial was concluded with the judge finding the accused not guilty. Dawn was devastated. After the trial she confronted her son's murderer and said to him, "you got off by this judge's verdict but there is another judge in Heaven that you will have to answer to!"

Stress or pressure can either crush or strengthen us; yet it strengthened Dawn's faith in Christ. When Dawn was baptized she said, "I am a work in progress." Her way of life was changing from dismal to optimistic. During the trial, our relationship changed from counselor/client to good friends it was then that Dawn started to call me mom.

A New Start

Dawn was interested in becoming a traffic controller, but she did not have enough money for the course. I contacted some friends regarding her situation and we put together enough money for her to take the course. She worked at this job for two and a half years. While she was working she realized that she needed more than just the stop paddle to control the traffic at night. Dawn designed a special glove that glowed in the dark; it was also useful during the day. She purchased a book on how to apply for a patent. She managed to fill out all the forms and now has a legal patent for her glove. I believe that one day her invention will be profitable.

Dawn has overcome exceptional trials throughout her life, but the one that still troubles her is the relationship with her daughter. Her constant prayer is that the Lord would intervene and bring healing in their relationship. Dawn longs for her daughter to forgive her so she can see her grandchildren. Dawn has a good relationship with her youngest son and she is proud of his accomplishments. He graduated from high school and is training to be a chef.

For many years, Dawn used anger and violence to survive. She is now learning to lean on her Heavenly Father to fight for her; He is her protector. I am sure, with the Lord's help, she will achieve whatever challenge is put before her because she knows that the Lord is with her and will never leave her.

"For I know the thoughts that I think towards you, says the LORD, thoughts of peace and not of evil, to give you a future and a hope. Then you will call upon Me and go and pray to Me, and I will listen to you. And you will seek Me and find Me, when you search for Me with all your heart." (Jeremiah 29:11-13)

I believe that the dark, painful days of Dawns life are over, and that the Lord has great plans ahead for her.

"The LORD your God is with you. He will take great delight in you, he will quiet you with his love, he will rejoice over you with singing". (Zephaniah 3:17)

I count it a privilege to have this feisty woman as one of my unofficial adopted daughters.

Chapter 10

The Drop-in Center

In 1995, I had a desire to establish a drop-in center for prostitutes that would be a safe place for counseling and support. Unfortunately, Crossfire Ministry could not afford to operate both a safe house and a drop-in center. After much prayer, the Lord opened a venue for us. In 1999, Gloria Keeler invited us to use her mission once a week. Living Waters Mission was on Hastings Street near Hawks. Thursday mornings, Vicky Zendugie and I would set up the mission, preparing hot soup, buns, coffee, and desserts. Before the women arrived we would walk around the area of Hastings and Cordova Streets, handing out invitations to the women for lunch. Most of the women had been out all night and were in rough shape; they were hungry, irritable, and desperate for a fix.

Living Waters Mission

It took a while before the women started attending the drop-in center because they thought that men would be there. When they learned that men were not allowed, they felt safe, and little by little the women trickled into the mission. The women were grateful for the hot soup and a warm quiet safe place to rest. It was not unusual to see a woman curled up on the couch fast asleep. As the women ate their lunch, we had many opportunities to pray for them and share the gospel.

Gloria Keeler offered us the use of her mission for a Christmas party, for the women. Gloria decorated the room and set up all the tables and chairs. Crossfire's team prepared lots of turkey, stuffing, mashed potatoes, vegetables, gravy, dessert, and gifts for the women.

Much to our surprise, approximately forty women attended. All the women were astounded that this dinner was just for them. Some of the residents from Crossfire's safe house helped serve the dinner. We sang Christmas songs, and the residents from the safe house gave their testimony of God's mercy in their lives. This was a very special night with lots of joy and love flowing throughout the room. As the women left they hugged us and told us how much they appreciated the party. We had many delightful years at this drop-in center building relationships with the women who worked in prostitution during the day time.

God Provides Helpers

Being a missionary to prostitutes and addicts is not a nine to five job, it is a twenty four hour job, seven days a week job. During my second year in the ministry, I became overwhelmed with so many women needing counseling and support. I prayed that the Lord would send dedicated Christian women to assist me. I am so thankful for Gail McFarland, Violet Wharton, Shirley Otto, and Judy Slootweg and many other volunteers. These wonderful godly women had the gift of love, compassion, and patience. Each woman had a strong commitment to minister to the needs of broken and traumatized women. I am sure that these volunteers have many of their own stories to share regarding their interaction with prostitutes.

Once a woman leaves prostitution she requires ongoing spiritual guidance, encouragement, and direction. The majority of the women who were addicts did not have the capability to cope with the daily stresses of life; they would become agitated over small issues and disappointments.

Many ex- prostitutes find it very difficult to cross the threshold into every day society; therefore it is necessary to assist them in building a new foundation for their lives. Most of the women had poor education and poor job skills.

When an addict becomes sober they become aware of the path of destruction they left behind. They have burnt bridges with family, friends, children, social workers and other government agencies; it often takes years to rebuild these bridges. Guilt and shame were often their adversary and caused them to sabotage their success by relapsing.

My expectations for recovering prostitutes and addicts had to be realistic as well as having faith that the Lord would transform their lives, and restore all the years that they had wasted. *"So I will restore to you the years that the locust has eaten." (Joel 2:25)* Many women found it difficult believing that God loved them and would forgive them. It was essential for me to continually build up their self-esteem, faith, and security in the Lord.

Who are They?

Over the years I encountered hundreds of young men and women who had lost their childhood innocence and self-esteem; they were broken hearted. They were people from all social, economic, and cultural backgrounds. They were targeted and recruited into the sex trade by unscrupulous men and women. Some ran away from home to escape mistreatment or other problems. Homeless, they started trading sexual favours for survival or for drugs and or alcohol. Addiction to drugs and alcohol is another factor that has been a linked to prostitution. The majority of these young people were molested when they were children.

Some people in our society see these young people as trash or a lost cause, but who are we to judge these young men and women?

Sexually Exploited

How could I judge a young woman who wept in my arms as she told me she had been raped by her father, who was supposed to be a Christian man? The anger, in this young woman was all consuming. The only way she could cope was through drugs, and the only way to support her habit was prostitution. Mercifully, this young woman received Jesus as her Saviour. She attended Christian counseling and found emotional healing and peace with God. She is now married and has a child.

A young First Nation's man, from Winnipeg, was raped by his uncle who had been his hero. His family would not accept his story. Not only did they reject his report about his uncle, but they also mocked him. He finally ran away to Vancouver. As a street kid, he started drinking and using drugs; he eventually ended up in prostitution.

Abandoned

A First Nation young woman was abandoned in the woods by her mother at the age of five. She was left to die with her twin sister and three year old brother. The two girls lived but the boy died. This tragedy never left her memory; she had continual nightmares of the incident. She felt guilty that she could not keep her brother alive. This dear young woman has spent years in and out of detox centers and recovery homes.

The Johns

You may ask, "What about the men who use prostitutes? Who are these men who buy sex?" They are called Johns. Some of them are ordinary lonely men, some are professional men, some have sexual addictions, and some are violent and abusive; they get their kicks out of beating a women and even killing them. It is sad that society judges prostitutes but ignores the men who purchase sex. Who is the greater sinner the prostitute or the John? *"For all have sinned and fall short of the glory of God." (Romans 3:23)*

My time ministering to prostitutes was interesting and challenging. God always had new experiences or encounters for me. One evening while I was talking with a transsexual man, I decided to sit down on the curb beside him. We were chatting when a car drove up and stopped. The man in the car wanted to talk to the woman in the pink pants. I looked around and realized that was me. The transsexual man jumped up and started to yell at the man to leave me alone. It was so funny that I laughed and laughed until I almost fell off the curb.

You might think that I am a bleeding heart and perhaps, I am. I know when I was being lied to or manipulated; it didn't upset me, because my job was to love these lost women and men and give them hope and lead them to Jesus.

My memory is full of many stories I have heard over the years, stories of heartbroken people who have had their childhood stolen from them. Their lives became distorted and dysfunctional but God in His infinite love died for each one and welcomes them into His kingdom. He puts the robe of righteousness on them and welcomes them to His banqueting table. I often got letters and phone calls, from family members, thanking Crossfire Ministries for rescuing their daughters and sending them home. Some of these phone calls have come from, Ontario, Winnipeg, Calgary, Seattle and other parts of the United States.

I believe that during the fifteen years of ministering to prostitutes, approximately two hundred or more left prostitution; they are now living with their families leading normal lives. Their lives are so changed that you would never recognize them as an ex-prostitute. They attend your church; they work beside you in your work place, and serve you at your bank or government office.

The love and mercy of Jesus profoundly impacted my life as I witnessed how He dealt with their sin, brokenness and healed their lives. Jesus sees them as lost sheep that have been wounded and left to die. I am sure Jesus walked with me through the dark streets of Vancouver pouring out His love and compassion.

Who are these women? They are the woman caught in adultery, *(John 8: 3-10)* the woman at the well. *(John 4: 7-25)* They are the people invited to the great supper after others refused to attend. *"The servant returned and told his master what they had said. His master said, 'Go quickly into the streets and alleys of the city and invite the poor, the crippled, and lame and the blind.' After the servant had done this, he reported, 'There is still room for more.' So his master said, "Go out into the country lanes and behind the hedges and urge anyone you find to come, so that the house will be full." (Luke 14:21-23)*

When you see a young person who has lost their way, please pray for them and share the love of Jesus with them because He died for these lost sheep. The church's mandate is to share the good news of the gospel and set the prisoners free whether the prisoner is your family, neighbor, business man, or prostitute; there is no distinction. We are called to love God, one another, and the world.

"And Jesus came and spoke to them saying. All authority has been given

to Me in heaven and on the earth. Go therefore and make disciples of all the nations, baptizing them in the name of the Father and of the Son and of the Holy Spirit. Teaching them to observe all things that I have commanded you; and lo, I am with you always even to the end of the age." (Matthew 28:18)

My prayer is that the Church will actively seek and save the lost throughout the whole world.

Crossfire Ministries was in opperation from 1987-2004. During that time much good was achieved because of Jesus who transforms lives.

*Scripture References from the New American Standard and the New King James Version

Resources for Recovery

Vancouver Detox

377 East 2nd Avenue, Vancouver BC, V5T 1B9

Phone: 1 (866) 658 1221

Hope for Freedom Society – Glory house for Women

3237 Liverpool Street Port Coquitlam BC, V3B 3V5

Phone: (604) 464 0472

Heartwood Centre for Women with Addictions

4500 Oak Street Vancouver BC, V6H 3N1

Phone: (604) 875 2026 Toll free 1 888 300 3088

Women into Healing

Alcohol and Drug Rehab Treatment Centre in Vancouver

Phone: (604) 477 1152

New Dawn Recovery Home for Women

720 King Edward Avenue East, Vancouver BC

Phone: (604) 325 0576

Servants Anonymous Society

201 7452 Street Surrey BC, V3W 4W7

Phone: (604) 590 23 04

Servants Anonymous Society offers a safe secure homes, education and addiction programs, long term support, hope and wholeness to female youth and women who have been sexually exploited and are homeless and or are at risk of homelessness and exploitation.

BC Teen Challenge

For women 19 and older

Phone: (604) 575 3930 or 1 (888) 575 3930

Union Gospel Mission

Day Shelter for Women 9am to 5:30 pm Monday to Friday

Phone: (604) 253 3323

Orchard Recovery Center

811 Grafton Road Bowen Island BC, V0N 1G2

Phone: (604) 312 9308

Crossroads Treatment Centre

123 Franklyn Road Kelowna BC V1X 6A9

Phone: Toll Free 1 (866) 860 4001 or 1 (250) 860 4001

Crisis Pregnancy Centre

#203 1070 Ridgeway Avenue, Coquitlam BC, V3J 1S7

Vancouver - Phone: (604) 731 1122

Burnaby - Phone: (604) 525 0999

Maple Ridge - Phone: (604) 463 5513

Surrey - Phone: (604) 584 4490

Aldergrove - Phone: (604) 856 9151

Women Against Violence Against Women

Rape Crises Phone (877) 392 7583 or (604) 255 6344

Made in the USA
Charleston, SC
06 March 2014